Praise

"*Snapshots* is not just a series of delicious stories. Nor is it a delicious cookbook. It is both, and more. Sandra Martin's collection of vignettes from her remarkable life feels like the sun—whole worlds have revolved around Sandra in a perfectly natural way. Riveting, engrossing, and delightful."

Dean Radin, PhD, Chief Scientist at the
Institute of Noetic Sciences (IONS)

"Sandra shared delicious recipes and revealed a few of her psychic experiences along her spiritual journey. Yes, a few of the stories were laugh out loud funny. She's a game-changer for sure. A great read."

Loretta LaRoche, Author and Stress Management Consultant

"We break bread with friends and form life-long bonds over the dinner table. Sandra Martin does the same with this book. She pulls you into her stories and holds you there while feeding you like a mother feeds her family, with joy, laughter, tears and sometimes just makes you hold your breath. Will she survive to the end of the page? Life explodes when extraordinary events happen to ordinary people, but then, Martin is not ordinary. *Snapshots* proves to be a phenomenal book that cannot be copied like a recipe, only savored like a fine table."

Arlene S. Bice, Author, Speaker, Teacher of Poetry,
Memoir, and Metaphysics

"Sandra has cooked up a perfect masterpiece! She takes a dash of spirituality, mixes it together with a zest for life and creates genuine recipes to nurture the body, and feed the soul! I want another course!"

James Van Praagh, Author of New York Times *bestseller,* Talking to Heaven, *producer of* The Ghost Whisper *and* Spiritual Medium

"Sandra Martin has served up an engaging consommé of vignettes from her extraordinary life as a literary agent, producer and world traveler that will tickle, titillate and stimulate the reader...and the recipes aren't bad either!"

Jim Marrs, New York Times *Best-selling Author*

"Sandra Martin offers us a delectable meditation on life, spirituality, and wholesome food. Be prepared to laugh, cry and feast on her multisensory observations from her garden to her kitchen to her times in the front row of the human potential movement. Her recipes for dinner and for life are rich and savory. Bon appetite."

Marilyn Schlitz, Social Anthropologist, Research and Award-Winning Writer

"*Snapshots* is a combination of light-hearted and soul-bearing stories. Sandra's life mission to bring love, light and true knowledge was a game-changer to the publishing and television worlds. Her determination to make this information available to a larger audience was arduous but she persevered. And I'm glad she did. I highly recommend this entertaining and important book."

Gary Renard, the Best-selling Author of The Disappearance of the Universe *trilogy*

"My good friend, Sandra Martin, has written a delightful book. It is full of wisdom and useful information. It is a perfect complement to most any evening and should be best enjoyed with a glass of your favorite wine or beverage. Thank you Sandra for sharing your stories."

Bill Hayes, President Figure 8 Films

"Sandra is really cooking in these smart, often funny, adventure stories in the life of a literary agent. Will the scent of roasted vegetables herewith remind you, a la Proust, of her plane crash in the Grand Canyon? Celebrity encounters, magical coincidences, transcendent thoughts and, yes, comforting eats, Sandra delivers it all."

Patrick Huyghe, Author of The Field Guide to Extraterrestrials *and* Columbus Was Last

"Sandra has written a wise and witty book, one that demonstrates that true wisdom comes from simply living life, not from listening to obscure teachings, and that meaning is created through the little experiences we have along the way, not as a thunderbolt out of the blue. Sandra's life has been well lived and she speaks as an elder of many pathways. Beautiful book."

Jim Garrison, President Wisdom University

"A combination of fascinating anecdotes describing some of the lively episodes of Sandra Martin's life from growing up on a tobacco and dairy farm in rural Virginia to a successful career as a literary agent in New York City promoting "New Age" authors, coupled with tempting personal recipes for everything from Spinach Lasagna to Roasted Salmon. A great read!

Jane Hughes Gignoux, Author of Some Folks Say: Stories of Life, Death, and Beyond

"Personal stories, well told and deliciously human, add flavors to Sandra Martin's new cookbook that cannot be found on a grocery shelf. They come from the human heart and soul, and accompany recipes that are as varied and tasty as life itself."

Catherine Nixon Cooke, Author of Tom Slick Mystery Hunter *and former president of the Mind Science Foundation.*

Snapshots: Memories and Recipes

Copyright © 2016 by Sandra Martin

No part of this publication may be reproduced, or stored in a retrieval system, or transmitted in any form or by any means, mechanical, recording or otherwise, without the express written permission of the copyright holder.

Publisher: Lisa Hagan Books
Design: Smythtype Design
Illustrations MattGrove/istock; LokFung/istock; knopazyzy/istock; Ievgeniia Lytvynovych/istock

ISBN-13: 978-0-9974699-3-6

Printed in U.S.A

Snapshots
Memories & Recipes

Heart wrenching, magical, funny, romantic: stories of my life.

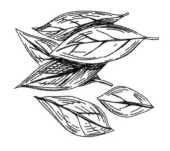

Sandra Martin

LISA HAGAN BOOKS

DEDICATED TO
Thomas Staples Martin
Florence Ferrell Martin

Table of Contents

Introduction
Snapshots: Memories and Recipes

When Lisa, my daughter, asked me if I'd write a cookbook for her new publishing imprint, Lisa Hagan Books, I hesitated. She stood there in front of me, hands on hips, superman style, and issued her challenge: "You always say no to everything; just think about it is all I'm asking." Who, me? Write a cookbook? I never cook by following a recipe! I'm the last person to write a cookbook. For me a recipe is a suggestion, a structure, a beginning.

Like most cooks, I do have my own tattered spiral bound note book in which I'd made notations about exceptionally good recipes that got lots of compliments. Plus those recipes that just kind of came to me, based on what was fresh in the garden, or what was in the refrigerator and in the pantry. Also included were the recipes that I'd had at friend's homes and restaurant dinners that were exceptional; meals I wanted to remember and re-create. Slowly I realized there was a treasure in that battered note book. I began to spend some time thinking about what kind of a book I could write that'd make both of us happy.

When Lisa came by again, I offered to write a book of recipes but with stories to go with them. I had a lot of stories. Mine was a lifetime of hard-knocks, magical happenings, sweet romances and some funny stories. She thought that was a great idea.

I spent six months testing recipes that I thought were appropriate for a cookbook. It was a tasty time and I enjoyed the process. During that time I also worked on the stories. I'll admit creating the recipes was the harder of the two.

Growing up on the Farm

I grew up on a tobacco and dairy farm in rural Southside Virginia where everyone had vegetable gardens. Planting, weeding and harvesting the garden imbued, infused, and forever left me with a love of fresh vegetables. Most summer mornings, I'd walk out to the garden, the screen door slamming behind me, shoes wet with dew, bucket in my hand, then squatting down low, inching along picking butter beans, or snaps or peas while humming "Puppy Love" or "Amazing Grace" or daydreaming, mostly daydreaming. Most of my daydreams were about how to get off the farm and move into town.

Our mainstays were butter beans, yellow squash, green beans, tomatoes, cucumbers, potatoes, back-eyed peas, cabbage and corn. Butterbeans were my favorite. I enjoyed the full farm-to-table process. After picking and shelling the butterbeans I'd quickly throw them into the pot to cook. When they were done, I'd pour off some of the liquid, then add a little salt, pepper, butter and serve with fresh-out-of-the garden, cut-up, juicy tomatoes with a little sugar or a lot of sugar depending on who made them, to take the edge off the acid. What a treat.

That was every summer of my young life. I was the eldest of four and we worked hard on the farm. We grew tobacco and grains and we had a dairy with Holstein cows. Every morning a pitcher of milk straight from the cow was brought to the house. As I look back at it now, it was a magical way to grow up; knowing where the food came from, canning or freezing what we'd be eating all winter. Come fall we'd have the basement stocked with Irish potatoes and sweet potatoes. We'd even have green tomatoes turning red in the basement until after Thanksgiving.

Dad and neighbors butchered and killed pigs and cows. Mom and I killed and dressed chickens. That was a messy, smelly business.

So much so that it is a wonder that I ate meat at all and it is a wonder that I eat it now. I spent a long, happy time as a vegetarian when I was young, first married and had discovered yoga. I was raising two kids, had a full time office job and to satisfy my extremely creative self, crafting everything in sight. It was a very stressful but fulfilling life. Then one Saturday morning, standing in my minuscule suburban kitchen I had such an overwhelming desire for steak that I, as if hypnotized, got in the car, drove to Safeway, fast-walked to the back of the store, got myself a big T-bone steak, brought it home, took it out of the package, slapped it in a pan, and cooked it right that minute. I stood over the stove while it barely cooked and then I ate the whole thing, straight out of the pan. It was beyond delicious. There went my vegetarianism.

Still it was vegetables that spoke to my heart.

After many years as a literary agent in New York City, I moved back to the farm I grew up on. What a blessing that was and is. As an agent I mainly represented manuscripts on consciousness, self-help, spirituality, parapsychology, alternative health, dreams, near-death, astrology, ancient mysteries, UFOs and conspiracies. For over 15 years I attended every conference on these subjects, met and talked with every speaker that interested me. I met almost everyone who had something original to say and wanted to write a book. Some of them became my clients, then household names and celebrities. I said no thank you to potential clients even more often and often they, too, became household names.

At first, metaphysics or New Age, as it was called then, was a broad genre, encompassing everything from psychic development to deep mysticism. It was also a genre that had been sidelined and never featured in bookstores. Over the years I spent representing clients in the genre, it became mainstreamed: alternative health books finally made it into the "Health" section; new spirituality shifted into "Spirituality"; and dream interpretation, intuition and all sorts of similar subjects were shelved in a new section deemed "Self-Help." Parapsychology books never made it to the "Science" section of bookstores. Many books on subjects such as UFOs, Ancient Mysteries, and Conspiracies are still housed in the Occult and/or New Age section of bookstores.

I will always be grateful for the seekers of all types who told me their stories, whether I took them on as clients or not. I have never met more interesting, more provocative, driven and excited writers. I loved every day of it. I loved their stories and felt strongly I was privileged to be part of sharing their wisdom, exploring new concepts, and investigating ancient mysteries.

It was an awesome life, but I was ready to retire. I lived on the 35th floor of a high-rise on 57th Street in Manhattan and life was good but stressful. I was ready for a change of pace.

My new home on Lake Gaston was serene and meditative. Friends from Manhattan said I'd never be happy without the wild craziness of my life and business in New York City. They were wrong. I loved getting back to the farm, slowing down, and of course entertaining all the friends from New York City who drove down, flew down and trained down to see what the heck I was doing.

Some came and stayed and stayed. Some gave it a day and night and shot right back to the city. One, a real New Yorker, wandered bleary eyed into the kitchen after her first night in my guest room. I asked her how she slept and she said, "Sleep! I didn't close my eyes all night. I've never been so scared. It was so dark I couldn't see my hand in front of my face and then absolute silence punctuated by weird sounds; whatever were those strange sounds?"

"Frogs in the water garden, birds flying over the lake and in the trees, animals marching through my yard. Who knows?"

She never came back.

As I re-acquainted myself with childhood friends I was also busy meeting my new neighbors. We called them "Lake" people as opposed to "local" people. Lake Gaston was built on the Roanoke River in 1963. It is thirty four miles long and has about 350 miles of shoreline. It has hundreds of subdivisions in Mecklenburg County and Brunswick County in Virginia and in North Carolina's counties for retirement homes and vacation homes. There are an estimated 150,000 people in the immediate area, so I'm told. These new residents are mostly retired business people, successful and accomplished additions to the neighborhood. I found that many of these new friends were eager to widen their spiritual search for a deeper meaning and a broader understanding of why we are here. Many were already studying our spiritual and self-help books.

The following stories define the foundation and impetus for my spiritual and metaphysical journey. There are a few pieces about my early life and my years in Richmond and Virginia Beach. Also included are stories from Manhattan and my travels around the world. These pieces are fundamentally about the structure from which I have built my life, my goals, my spiritual search, and my career.

I've written in journals since the late 1960s so I have a day-by-day chronicle of my life; much of it totally boring. When I read those early journals I wonder who that young woman was and I am awed and amazed at her conviction and the belief that she could do anything she set her mind to.

At the end of each story is a recipe of fresh from-the-garden vegetables or dishes I had at various restaurants or friends homes that I liked so much I created my own version. These are tried and true recipes that I can depend on being a hit with my guests. All of the recipes are easy to follow and most don't take more than 30 minutes to prepare.

I offer these stories to you as parables about life, about the hard path, the intuitive path and the deeply spiritual one. Some stories are just funny.

All of my life I've cooked and I have loved serving friends and family nourishing, delicious, and satisfying meals. Cooking feeds the body and the conversation around a table of good friends feeds the soul. Nurturing others has always been a natural part of who I am.

I hope you'll enjoy my stories and my recipes.

A Meditation Experience
Leek and Potato Soup

As a young, married suburban woman in Richmond, Virginia, I was in a spiritual quandary and on such an intense spiritual search that I tried just about anything. I was desperate to discover what life was about, what it meant, who I "really" was and why I was here. I was in my early 20s with two children. Somehow I knew that this current 'me' wasn't all that I was meant to be. I investigated all the mainstream religions, attended weekly prayer groups. Even though I'd been brought up Primitive Baptist I tried out a Catholic Charismatic group and was invited to not come back. I kept saying, "Do you really think that is what Jesus would say?" Apparently we weren't supposed to question the priest.

I also explored all sorts of alternative thought systems, from Madame Blavatsky's Theosophy to Edgar Cayce's Search for God Study Groups and George Ritchie's Universal Youth Core. After all, it was *the* 60s and even though I was a suburban Mom married to an accountant, I wasn't totally unaware of the vast changes going on in the world.

As part of my exploration, I began to take yoga classes. Back in the 60s and 70s yoga was a spiritual practice, not a source for physical exercise. There were no yoga mats; we brought towels from home. No special clothes or water bottles, either. It was just us and the teacher. The classes were taught in a townhouse a few blocks off the campus of the Virginia Commonwealth University (VCU) by an English professor. She'd light incense and candles. She created a warm, safe, loving environment.

Marcia was an extremely beautiful, dark eyed, statuesque brunette. She had a strong physical presence, but a breathy Marilyn Monroe come-hither voice. Her voice was always a surprise. It could have been the spiritual manifestation of opposites. After teaching all day, being in charge, the soul of power, at night she turned into a receptive and non-threatening whisper of a person, the soul of submissiveness. Or maybe it was because she was over six feet tall and a formidable person and this was her way of not overwhelming us. She was a mystery and a fascination to me. I went every Wednesday night at 7 PM.

I took to yoga like a duck to water. My body was young, supple and the postures felt natural. The meditation was even better. As a Primitive Baptist in a small southern Virginia town, yoga wasn't in our vocabulary. And if it had come up, it would've been reason for serious concern. It might have even been cause for a call to the minister.

I was very quiet; I don't think I ever spoke except to chant the mantra for meditation. I did the yoga poses easily, eagerly waiting for the meditation. Marcia's voice took us on a long whispery voyage, an incantation that took us down, down into our deeper selves to reach for our highest spiritual inclinations. I loved it. It felt to me to be a superior way of discovering my higher self, a self that I been searching for—one full of respect and belief in this vast universal part of me connected to all of mankind.

This one meditation, the reason I'm writing, took place after we were deep into our inner worlds. We'd finished our exercises and Marcia led us into a meditation. I was sailing along on the OM vibe and felt a change in the energy around me. I opened my eyes and suddenly I wasn't sitting in a Grove Avenue townhouse. I was looking out of eyes in another world. I was high up in mountains, vast mountains, and overwhelming endless vistas beyond my astonished eyes. No snow, just grey; grey skies, grey rocky cliffs. A deep sense of peace penetrated my every cell. Where was I? What was this? I was nervous, scared, excited and calm at the same moment.

Then I looked down and discovered that I wasn't in my body. Oddly, this didn't seem to upset me at all. My/his legs were brown, thin and so skinny, I could see the bones, and these legs were unbelievably dirty legs.

All of a sudden I became aware of HIM. I was surprised by a slightly humorous charm, his giggling energy and the genuine warmth that came from him. "We" were sitting on the ground. The ground was grey, rocky and cold. One small dented pan, a battered wooden box and nothing else. I blinked trying to figure out what was happening. He laughed inside. His sweet peace was all encompassing. I shut my eyes again, letting this anxiety-less world envelop me. I relaxed into it. I breathed into it.

After a while I started to get slightly worried about the Grove Avenue yoga studio and how to get back there. I could feel the hard stones under his almost naked bottom. I could feel the emptiness of his stomach. His dry mouth. I knew he lived slightly down and to the left in a small cave. I wondered if he was on Grove Avenue checking out the yoga class. I somehow knew that this was Tibet and he was an ascetic monk. Even though he was a warm and inviting presence I was ready to go back home. But how? I decided that I had to go back into deep meditation. I focused my energy, filled my being with OM and descended into my center.

Moments later, I somehow knew I was back in Richmond. I opened my eyes and was surprised to see that everyone else had packed up and left, except Marcia. She was sitting near me in a meditative state. Maybe she was participating with me. I don't know. She asked if I was okay and I told her what had happened.

She said sometimes things like that happen when you go deep into meditation. You're blessed, she told me.

I drove the 30 minutes back to the suburbs in a daze. My mind was traveling from one world to another trying hard to anchor in my body.

I've never forgotten that experience and that man.

I wonder if he remembers me.

That first experience deepened my understanding of the mind and how un-tethered we are if we really let go. How sweet the freedom from the body could be and that experience encouraged me to continue to dig deep into understanding why we're here and what it all means. As if anyone could actually ever know anything for certain, for sure.

But soup always soothes the questioning spirit and I have always made soups like this one.

Leek and Potato Soup

4 leeks; wash and clean them well; slice them thinly, the
  white part with a little green for color

3 tablespoons unsalted butter

2 thyme sprigs

1 bay leaf

Salt to taste

1 pound of yellow potatoes, peeled, quartered and sliced

6 cups water

1/2 cup heavy cream

1. Melt the butter over medium heat in a heavy bottomed pot.
2. Add the leeks along with thyme, bay leaf and salt.
3. Add the potatoes and cook for 4 or 5 minutes stirring to spread the flavor.
4. Add the water and bring to a boil. Simmer for about 25 minutes.
5. When done, stir in cream.
6. Salt and pepper to taste.
5. Remove bay leaf and thyme sprigs.

Serve.

Life Happens
Salmon with Dill

While raising young children, taking care of the family and taking yoga I also took a job at an advertising agency as a receptionist. I wasn't even 20 years old. When I look back on it now, everything that happened at that agency could've been inserted directly onto AMC's *Mad Men* television series. The fictional series is set in 1960s New York and, although I was in Richmond, Virginia, there was no difference in the way women were treated. That television series was so true to the 60s that, for me, it was unsettling watching it.

It was a very small agency; we had a few national clients, but mostly local advertising accounts. And we had our own Don Draper. He looked the same, talked the same, and he lived a fast and dangerous life.

Life at that long narrow building on the corner of a big empty parking lot was soap opera central. The owner, I'll call him Donnie, had a neurotic and very scary secretary. She was tall, very skinny and not in a good way, had stringy hair that always needed combing, and was edgy, and easily flustered. She, in turn, had a very handsome, mysterious and strange boyfriend who drove her to work, picked her up for lunch, deposited her back and showed up to take her home. He rarely spoke. She was given to screaming fits, crying for no apparent reason and telling lies. Outrageous lies that everyone knew were lies but no one, I mean no one, ever called her on. I realize now since watching *Mad Men* it was the weight of knowing all of Donnie's secrets and having to keep them from his wife that contributed to her extreme mood swings. I'm just guessing, of course. She could've just been crazy.

Donnie was tall, dark and handsome with slicked back hair just like Don Draper. He smoked a pipe; he wore fine clothes and was very smart about advertising. He knew every angle, every shortcut to success and he took them all. We used to say; "That Donnie, he's a smooth operator."

All the employees were aware of Donnie's mistress. She was young, cute and she lived in the apartment building, across the parking lot directly behind our building. He'd come to work, late mornings, walk through the building, getting an update from each department and issuing orders; copy, production, art and straight on out the back door to spend the day with *her*. The building was just behind the office and he always went into the rear entrance. If he made it back to the office in the afternoon he'd have a short glass of bourbon with him and he'd be feeling no pain.

The production manager was another cover person for Donnie. He'd always take Donnie's calls; yes, he is busy with another client, at a production meeting, working with the art department, etc. What can I do to help you?

He never let on Donnie was in the apartment building behind us having wild sex. At least that is what I always thought.

I started out at the agency as the receptionist, moved quickly to copy proof reader, then to writing copy. The copywriter was smart, sweet and a severe alcoholic. Every morning he came to work with bloodshot eyes and smelled like an alcohol factory. Some mornings on Donnie's tour through the building, he told him to go home and sleep it off. Even though the copywriter had his problems, he was a generous spirit who gave me the opportunity to move up in the organization. Of course, he always took credit for my work but that was the way it was then.

My office was small and the copy machine was in my office. That was another parallel to *Mad Men*; the new girl copywriter has the copy machine in her office, too. Another employee was this twitchy, nervous, innocent older woman who we wouldn't let in my office because she'd make the copy machine go wacky every time. Even if she stepped inside the doorway it'd act up. It got so she'd stand just outside the doorway and whoever was making copies would take her papers and copy them for her, hand them back to her and sigh. This was my first experience with psychokinetic energy.

This was the 60s and so many people were really changing in revolutionary ways—but women were treated poorly even by revolutionaries. It had always been this way. Looking back on it I am amazed that we women took it for so long. Men really treated us like objects and spoke to us as lesser human beings. Because the company was always trying to save money and because I was young and cute, they used me in many ad and marketing campaigns. If they used me they didn't have to pay a model or an actress a fee. In one ad I was posed on a ladder to hype plumbing fixtures and the guys were all gathered below. I was uneasy because I knew they were looking up my very short dress and having a great old time. But what to do? I felt, as every woman in America did at that time, that I had no recourse.

Thank God for the women's movement and Eleanor Roosevelt. When Jack Kennedy was running for President, he went to Eleanor to ask for her blessing. She told him she didn't approve of him and his womanizing ways but she'd give him her blessing if he'd start a new government department to study equality between men and women. This department eventually became the National Organization for Women (NOW). They found that, in the 60s, women made 23 cents for every dollar a man made doing the same work and, oh Lord, we've come so far! Now we make 72 cents for every dollar a man makes. And that great leap has only taken 50 years!

But I digress. Donnie had his schedule set pretty strictly and he followed it faithfully. We covered when necessary. His wife called quite often to check on him; she being no fool. She was gracious and southern and introduced him to all the best families in Virginia. She was old Virginia stock and he was the new boy in town. But she knew something was going on. Whenever she called, his secretary would call Donnie at the mistress's apartment behind us and he'd call the wife. A well-oiled machine.

Until.

Late one afternoon I took the mail out to the mail box that was right in front of the office building and I heard music. I peeked around the corner of the building and there was the wife's Lincoln Continental, parked next to Donnie's Lincoln Continental. Perfectly coiffed, perfect make up and beautiful as always. Door open, radio on, music playing, she was sitting in the passenger seat with a martini shaker by her side, a martini glass in one hand, a cigarette in the other. And on her lap was a shiny black gun.

She had her eye on the back door of the apartment building. She didn't see me. Thank goodness. Oh my God? What to do?

I scooted back into the office in a panic. We were so used to covering for him, it didn't occur to me that he deserved what he was about to get. I stood in the lobby not knowing which way to go. To the right was the secretary. No, no, not the secretary because who knew what she'd do. She was made of highly flammable material and the least thing would set her off. I took off down the hall to the left.

I knocked on the production manager's office door. I knew he was the one to take care of this impending disaster. He was small, frumpy, with heavy black framed eye glasses and he always said "no" while he rotated his left shoulder in obedience to some strange nervous habit. Negative was his only mode. The production manager had someone in his office and ignored me. I kept trying to interrupt but he motioned me go away. I knew I had to persist. Finally, he came out in to the hallway, his eyes blazing and angry. I tell him quickly that the wife is outside the building with a gun waiting for Donnie.

His eyes wide with panic, he sprinted down the hall to an empty office and made a phone call.

About 10 minutes later, Donnie rushed in through the front door. Donnie had obviously walked out of the front door of his lover's apartment building and around the entire block to come through the front door of the office. He'd avoided the back apartment entrance where his wife, parked directly across from it, would've seen him. He and the production manager conferred. They never asked me anything; never looked my way, and never even acknowledged my part in this potentially exploding drama.

After conferring, Donnie casually walked outside to his wife's car and asked, "What on earth are you doing?" She who gave him four beautiful children and still looked like a prom queen jerked her head around at his voice. She is shocked to see him behind her instead of coming out the back entrance of the apartment building. They walked back inside together. No ugly scenes out on the street.

Together they go in to his office. The door is open. It is directly across from me. I hear every word, see every move.

She says she knows he is seeing someone else. She says she has been watching him for days and she knows there is another woman. She says, I've seen you two together. Her movements and her voice are fragile and scared. This is the end of it, she says. She lifts the gun and points it shakily at her husband. Donnie confidently reaches out and takes the gun out of her hand. She doesn't even protest. He says you must've seen someone who looked like me; I've been here all day. The production manager, standing there beside them, confirms Donnie's story saying, "That's right, he's been in the office all day long." She ends up crying and saying she's been a fool. Donnie pulls her to him and hugs her all the while, behind her back, giving the production manager thumbs up while mouthing thank you.

It is never acknowledged or even mentioned that I was the one who saw her and reported her to the production manager. It was a sad day.

The next day, Donnie came in, did his customary tour of the office and high-tailed it out the back door. Nothing had changed.

Something fishy was happening at that ad agency all the time.

Salmon with Dill

¹/₂ pound salmon

¹/₄ cup chopped fresh dill

Juice of 1 lemon

¹/₄ cup olive oil

2 cups roughly chopped cauliflower

1 bunch leeks, white part and a little green cleaned and
   sliced thin

Salt and pepper to taste

Additional oil for cooking

1. Mix salt, pepper, dill, lemon juice together with ¹/₄ cup of
    olive oil.
2. Cover salmon with the olive oil mixture—seal in a plastic bag
    and refrigerate overnight.
3. The next day, preheat the oven to 350 degrees.
4. In a large fry pan, heat olive oil on high.
5. Add the cauliflower and leeks; decrease the heat to medium,
    and sauté until soft.
6. Take heavy aluminum foil and make a little packet; spoon the
    vegetables onto the bottom, put the salmon on top, seal the
    packet, and cook in the oven at 350 degrees for 20 minutes.

Serves 4.

The Grand Crash
Roasted Vegetables

In the early 70s I divorced. Then I really started having adventures. These experiences began when Lloyd, an old friend and a distinguished professor of Urban Planning at the University of Richmond, called to ask if I'd like to fly with him to San Francisco. I unhesitatingly said, "Yes!" Coming with us, he said, would be Nubuko, a Japanese exchange student. Nubuko was the opposite of what Americans thought of when they thought of Japanese women—she was assertive and sassy, determined not to be thought of as traditional. Nubuko was an adventurer. In Japan she was a Christian in a land of Buddhists.

The following weekend the three of us drove north out of Richmond to the woodsy, quiet Hanover Airport, and checked out the Mooney before our departure. The Mooney was rated as the most reliable single engine small plane built. The wings were low and you stepped up onto them to get inside. Every system on the plane checked out fine.

We loaded up and took off.

Lloyd was an excellent pilot and had been flying for over thirty years. He'd made this trip many times as he divided his life between San Francisco where he'd married, had kids, divorced and now Richmond, Virginia where he worked.

We flew from Richmond to Mississippi on the first leg, to Amarillo for the second leg, and then to Taos, where we stayed at the adobe home of a Richmond friend and worldly-wise airline stewardess. Her house was up in the mountains, nestled in a little grove of trees, with the irrigation ditch close by and a blazing garden. It was unlike anything I'd ever seen-except in Georgia O'Keefe art. We meant to leave after a day's visit but stayed for another day. We visited the Hopi Reservation and listened to water rights stories.

Reluctantly, we said goodbye to Taos to push on to our next destination, Las Vegas. The Mooney was a short hopper. We flew from small airport to small airport. Once while landing late at night, we rolled in on the grassy median between the asphalt runways and a man came out to meet us with a big gun in the crook of his arm. Another time we were avoiding thunderstorms and got lost. We saw a freeway, swooped down, and followed it until we reached our exit.

At the Taos airport we filed our flight plan. This is the only way the FAA can track you-in case something happens. Lloyd, leaning on the airport counter surrounded by maps, asked me, "Do you want to fly over the Grand Canyon or take the more direct route?"

"I've never wanted to see the Grand Canyon—definitely not, let's go the direct flight." In fact my inner voice was very definite about not wanting to go to the Canyon, fly over it or in any way get near it.

Nubuko, new in America, said, "I'd love to see the Grand Canyon. In fact, I want to see all the wonders of America."

Again, I insisted, "No, I don't want to go there."

"Sandra, it's so unlike you to be so vehement about anything, much less flying over one of the wonders of the world—what has happened to your southern gentility? This place is filled with geologic history." Lloyd was clearly surprised at my reaction; as was I. "You are usually so easy going, so southern and so polite." He gestured to our Japanese exchange student, and now fellow adventurer with an expression that said, "Aw, come on."

I felt very strongly that I didn't want see the Canyon, but had had so little experience with being assertive, I graciously gave in. Graciously giving in was something that I'd had a great deal of experience with all my life.

It took two false starts to get off the top of Taos Mountain. The updrafts were powerful. That little Mooney was a great plane though. Like the little engine that could, the Mooney was sweet, gentle and always ready for one more trip: it kept on trying. On our third try we were off and into the wild blue yonder.

Having flown many times before in small planes, and controlled the radio I was the navigator, never the pilot. Like the old saying, never the bride always the bridesmaid, I was always the navigator. I always meant to take lessons.

It was a perfect, cloudless, warm August day. We got to the rim of the Canyon in short order, flew right over the rim and down into the Canyon and proceeded to dip, first the right wing, then the left, so we'd have perfectly unobstructed views. Nubuko was ooing and ahhing in the back seat. I, on the other hand, was looking for our exact coordinates on the map and locating the next radio beacon. Finally the overwhelming beauty entranced me, too. What can you say about the Grand Canyon? It is magnificent. Words can't come close to describing the contrast of the age of humanity to the age and grandiosity of the Canyon. Each of us was overcome with the power of nature and captivated with the views outside the plane.

Then, suddenly, in a flash, the plane was filled with smoke. Black, acrid smoke.

Flames were leaping from the engine. The engine was sputtering. Lloyd grabbed the radio, shouting out, "Mayday, Mayday, Mayday! This is bravo-niner.." He called out our plane's registration and location adding, "We have a fire. We have a fire." Nukubo from the back seat started whimpering and crying.

Simultaneously, Lloyd and I looked at each other and had the same thought; this plane is going to blow up as soon as the fire gets to the gas tanks.

In those brief moments, for me, time slowed down. All movements were in slow motion. My mind was exquisitely aware of everything-the colors of the Canyon, the fear in Nukubo's crying and Lloyd's intensely professional, impassioned although scared voice. In this quiet, almost peaceful state of mind, even realizing that the plane was about to blow up, I never panicked. Almost in a meditative state, I had one clear thought—I never told my Dad how much I loved him. It became clear, in a flash, that the only thing that matters when you believe you are going to die is love-who you love and how you've loved, when you've withheld it and when it's been given freely. That is all that is important.

Then I just knew, completely and totally, as sure as I was of anything, we'd be okay. I tried to calm Nubuko. She had become hysterical. The fire went out and the smoke cleared from the cabin. We were in free fall. We weren't going to blow up but now we had no engine. Thank God, the Mooney is a small, delicate plane and so we were gliding—downward, but nonetheless gliding. Unfortunately, because of those wind drafts, we couldn't glide up and over the rim where we could land. We were quiet. The plane was quiet.

Lloyd, Nubuko, and I scanned the Canyon for a place to set the plane down. There is nowhere to land in the Canyon. No flat stretches at all, anywhere. To crash in the Canyon was maybe better than blowing up but not much better, we nervously agreed.

Finally, in the far distance, about halfway down the Canyon we spied a sort of shelf sticking out from the Canyon wall. It was equal to the level we were flying, so we thought if we could keep the plane up in the sky that high we could make a forced landing and maybe walk away.

By the power of God's blessing, our collective will to live, and maybe all three of us holding our breath we made it to the edge of the mesa. The mesa looked relatively clear from way out there; a mile or so back, but as we got closer and closer we discovered it was covered in huge red boulders.

I zipped Nubuko into Lloyd's leather garment bag and snuggled her down behind my seat so she'd be protected, as much as possible, and made sure our seat belts were tight. As we approached, Lloyd and I nervously laughed, listening to Nubuko crying and obviously praying through the leather garment bag. After five or six muffled Japanese words, we'd hear "Jesus," and a few more Japanese words and then "Mary."

Our forced landing was a little bumpy but we were okay. The plane finally came to a halt and I unzipped Nubuko and we ran from the plane—afraid again that it might blow up.

We looked at each other thankful to be alive. Lloyd kept grabbing us, hugging us, and making sure we were okay. Lloyd and I had a few cuts, but we had no broken bones. Our eyes were brimming over with tears.

Nubuko, on the other hand, looked like she'd been casually passing by. Thanks to that nice leather garment bag, there was not a scratch on her.

In those few moments while we were standing gawking at each other, we heard a voice echo down, from the sky, "Are you alright, down there?" It was like God was speaking to us. We turned like a trio of cartoon characters to see a Grand Canyon Tour Plane circling. We signaled that we had no broken bones and the pilot replied that help was on the way.

It was 11AM on a hot August day. We had no water, no food, and not even a piece of gum between us. What were we thinking? After exploring the mesa a bit we sat under the broken wing and told each other our life stories. I believe that each of us synthesized and refocused our beliefs right there.

I talked about love, ideals, and that there are no absolutes in life—we are not promised life from day to day but we take it for granted. I said that I believed in the good of humankind, in following my heart and consequently, living purely and living in the moment—not planning my life months, years ahead any longer. I wanted to live, see the world; try to make a difference in other people's lives.

Lloyd and Nobuko looked at me awkwardly. Our relationships were casual, easy going, nothing serious. I thought it'd give them freedom to speak more from their hearts if I said my deepest truest feelings. They were confused by my openness.

Lloyd was mainly concerned with what happened to the plane and took the entire engine apart to find that a simple oil hose had burst and caused the fire. Then he said he was going to move back to San Francisco to spend more time with his kids. He loved being an architect and was tired of teaching. He wanted to be more creative. On a more mundane level, he wondered if his insurance would pay for removing the plane from the Grand Canyon? It didn't.

Nubuko was worried that she'd never see her policeman father again. Her mother had passed away and she'd converted to Christianity against her father's wishes and had moved far away. She also declared she would never fly again. And she didn't.

We explored the mesa. It was about a half mile long and maybe quarter mile deep, the cliff to the top would be a difficult climb and we wondered how they'd get us out. We knew there was no way we could go down-it was one hellacious drop. In fact, we kept walking to the edge and looking down, each of us thinking our own thoughts about what could've happened. It was already really hot, but we knew that the temperature dropped to near freezing at night so we were eager to be out of there. We also thought the rescue team would be right along. By 9 PM that night, we were getting seriously worried, as well as tired, cold and hungry.

Around 10 we heard men's voices calling out to us and we leapt up, ran towards the U. S. Park Rangers who were running towards us. I hugged them. They gave us canteens of water and we drank them down. Afterwards, we decided that that water must've been in those canteens for weeks—it was nasty, metallic tasting but gloriously wet. We gathered our stuff (luckily, we were all light packers) and hiked out. Well, really we were pushed, pulled and dragged up that cliff. But we got to the top.

And when we did we were met by the Sheriff and the Deputy Sheriff of Grand Canyon County. We were dirty, cold, exhausted and scared. It was almost midnight. We crashed at 11 AM! They were sitting in their car with the heater on and when we dragged ourselves over the top, a man stepped out of the passenger side of the car—the driver saying to him, "Can you handle this, son?"

The driver was a big hefty guy and the one walking towards us was a double for Barney Fife from the Andy Griffin Show. His gun went down to his knee, with obvious implications, and he walked with a swagger. He met us halfway, looked us over and asked Lloyd, "You folks having some trouble?"

The Deputy said we had to fill out these forms for the FAA before we could be driven into town. Lloyd did. Nubuko and I got in the car, in a back seat with no handles and warmed up. The Park Rangers wished us well and drove off.

The Sheriff informed us that we were a long way from civilization. It was a very dark night. We started off down a rough timber road. The Sheriff was shining his spotlight into the woods as we drove along. We were exhausted and quiet. They were laconic.

Finally, I asked, "Why are you shining that light in the woods?" "Well, if I see a little ole doe, I'm going to jump out and shoot her." Gee, I thought, don't let our ordeal interrupt your survival needs or maybe that was his entertainment.

He ventured, "You folks crashing is the most exciting thing that's happened around here in a long time, years maybe. The last excitement was when I drove an old epileptic Indian to the hospital in Flagstaff." He also volunteered that if we'd had broken bones they'd flown a helicopter from Flagstaff to pick us up within the hour! If only we'd known our options.

We arrived at Desert Village. Never was I so glad to see people. It was almost 3 AM and we were big news there. More importantly, in a resort town where people book hotel rooms years in advance, they kept two rooms open for us. Nubuko and I fell into bed and slept like the dead. But we were alive.

That day I flew to Las Vegas and stayed with a friend. I arrived late and the next morning at breakfast I told her parents about my experience. Her father leaned forward, thinking about his own children I'm sure and said, "Just think, your children could have been without a Mother today." I cried for a long time with that realization.

For years I'd been on the spiritual path, meditating, doing yoga, studying the Bible, and attending Edgar Cayce Search for God groups. Dr. George Ritchie was my mentor and a great and loving teacher. After the Grand Crash I realized that my spiritual path was a mere shadow of what it could have been. I turned inward to discover my true gift.

Our friend had made us delicious vegetarian dishes while we were in Taos. So in her honor we'll have a recipe of vegetables from the garden.

Roasted Vegetables

2 cups 1/2 inch diced carrots,

2 cups 1/2 inch diced parsnips,

2 cups 1/2 inch diced butternut squash and

2 cups 1/2 inch diced peeled sweet potatoes

Herb mixture: leaves of fresh basil, sage and parsley,
    sprigs of rosemary, finely chopped

Olive oil to moisten

Salt and Pepper to taste

1. Preheat the oven to 400 degrees.
2. Put all the vegetables in a large bowl or pot.
3. Add the herbs.
4. Mix olive oil and moisten all.
5. Remove and spread across a baking sheet, adjusting salt and pepper to taste.
6. Roast on 400 degrees for 15 or 20 minutes or until tender.

Life Changing Seminars
Zucchini Muffins

A friend had recently returned from attending a seminar: one of those EST-like weeks. Werner Erhard's seminars were focused on intensive communication and self-empowerment. In 1977 I had seen a movie *Semi-Tough* starting Burt Reynolds and Kris Kristofferson and Burt's character attends a seminar called B.E.A.T. to break the bad habits that were holding him back; the ones keeping him from achieving his full potential. It was funny. Immediately after, many other similar seminar and workshops popped up and it was one of them my friend had attended. She was over the top. The seminar, she gushed, had "changed her life." She also told me I had to take the seminar. I was not very interested and said I'd done so much work on myself in the 60s and 70s with Dr. Ritchie that I felt pretty good about consciousness, awareness level and psychological inner work. She was so determined that she paid for a week in Washington D.C. near DuPont Circle for me to attend. Please, do it for me, she'd begged. It is my gift to you.

So what the heck, how bad could it be?

Pretty bad, as it turns out. Really, it was a nightmare.

Having attended many self-help seminars in Richmond and then in Virginia Beach at the A.R.E., Spiritual Frontiers, and all sorts of community groups with good intentions I thought this seminar would be similar.

Instead, this workshop was held in an old, dark and grungy hotel, and the teacher or trainer as he wanted to be called was full of bullshit and a real bully from the moment he took the stage. He was dark haired, dark eyed and buff, well dressed and full of intense, wired energy. He was parroting lessons from Napoleon Hill's *Think and Grow Rich*, Dale Carnegie's *How to Win Friends and Influence People*, with a little Scientology thrown in but not in a good way. It was all designed to break down people, destroy barriers and, if you were lucky, rebuild with new positive self-empowered material. He said things like you're here because you're failures, you have no life, and you're lost and looking for direction. There was big applause after that-led by the volunteers who worked for the organization. They were circled around the room and were called Assistant Leaders.

We were told in no uncertain terms that as trainees, we were required to stay all day long, every day, for the entirety of the seminar. The doors would be locked. And the commitment to endure would be enforced. Were we ready? All 200 of us stood and with one voice made a commitment to stay the course no matter what. Then we had to make a commitment to trust ourselves, as our best information came from within and not from outside forces. We didn't have to stand or say this out loud. The most important message we could possibly hear and it got no applause.

I'd read that EST used authoritarian trainers who enforced numerous meaningless rules. And this fellow was following that pattern. He'd ask for volunteers to talk about trust, commitment, responsibility, and then promptly ridiculed their replies. On that first day it seemed his goal was to get every person in the room to cry. From a quick survey of the participants before he began it seemed to me that people who were drawn to this type of seminar were looking for direction in life, feeling at loose ends and waiting for someone to tell them what to do.

Strange rules were enforced. There was tape on the floor for the chairs to line up and if you moved your chair, like I did so I could put my knee up, the trainer stopped his lecture, pointed at you—that'd be me—and reprimanded the offender for moving the chair. I moved it back exactly like it was supposed to be. That was my first encounter. I later read this often happened. There was no relaxing. It was a very tense day. Every day.

We did all sorts of exercises; things I'd done 10 years before with George Ritchie. Going within, having a one on one with your neighbor on your right or your left. Bonding. We were told to look into their eyes and say "I trust you." Meaning what I'm not sure, since after that he had us walking around the room in a two big circles, looking into the eyes of each person, as we passed each one by and saying, "I trust you" and to the next person, "I don't trust you." Just weird. Being judgmental for the sake of being judgmental. All of the processes were random, unlike the exercises with Dr. Ritchie, these had no context.

The larger message was good: everything has always been available to you. You are more than you know. But underneath the positive was a terribly negative message: what am I pretending to know or not to know. Because of this, everything that happens to me is my fault entirely.

Everything our trainer said led back to getting more training with the organization. You need us.

If you made comments about other ways of dealing with the subject of the moment the trainer always dismissed the comment with ridicule and often paradoxical logic. He'd say something that just didn't make sense but was impossible to respond to in a meaningful way.

Another encounter I had with our trainer was when we were given a handful of sticks similar to the children's game pick-up sticks, in fact they may have been one and the same. We were to arrange them into a particular shape. I'm pretty good with those kinds of things and our group of four completed the task rather quickly. One of the group yelled out, "We did it, we did it" and that little trainer guy came right over. Our group was expecting kudos but instead he asked who did this and they pointed right at me, "She did." Damn they were quick to turn! "Did you cheat?" he asked me. "How did you know how to do this?" He confronted me on every front about this silly little game. I just answered him honestly. No, I'm just good at these kinds of games. But I could tell that at that moment, I was marked. I was not falling into line, not buying into the groupthink. Plus I was one of the ones that kept asking questions about other ways of addressing issues.

There were exercises that meant to work on issues of parenting but seemed to make the group uneasy and most ended up giggling. One person towered over, acting as the parent, and the other one on the floor as the child and you were to say what you thought your parents should've said, should've done. It was another strange exercise out of context, with no real meaning. I was getting really tired of the way he was treating people and me in particular. I had been assigned a "Leadership Assistant" to help me.

We had the de rigueur falling backwards into others arms to learn trust; we had to tell our partner something that happened when we were children that embarrassed and hurt us; we had to mirror what we see in our partners eyes—because you know you can only mirror what is inside yourself; we had to psychically tune into our partner. Then we had to say why we felt we were losers/unsuccessful; and how empowered we already felt from our trainers lessons. There were selections of who was the least attractive in the group, the most rigid, and the one who was not emotionally open enough. It was a sad three days. And there were two more days to go.

Late in the afternoon of the third day we had an exercise that guided us into a meditation to envision our sacred, safe space along with two words to describe it. So I did that. Afterwards we were asked to say what our sacred space contained, where it was, things like that. Most of the attendees said it was a little cottage by a lake or at a grandmother's house where each child was always loved. The words love, acceptance and joy filtered through the room. I didn't get that message at all. So when my turn came I almost decided to lie and just "fall into line" but instead I stood up and told what my sacred, safe space was.

It was a building like the Parthenon in Greece, only more grand and beyond beautiful. It was filled with every communication device available so I could get information on anything or anyone I was interested in on earth and throughout the universe. My safe space was located out in space, beyond the earth, almost to the moon. I could see the earth below me and the ever expanding universe beyond. My words were: unlimited and all encompassing.

Silence.

I said, "I am leaving now."

"You can't leave. You made a commitment."

"Yes, I did, but I also committed to listening to my inner voice, my intuition and it says it is time for me to leave this place."

It was very dramatic.

While I was talking, he was walking. I headed towards the door and as he caught up to me he put his arm securely around my shoulders. Every eye was on us, all 400 eyes, and it put serious pressure on me to conform. I could feel it coming from every direction. But, I just couldn't buy into his psychological and emotional abuse. I understood that many were benefiting from the process. I knew, from firsthand experience, that there were better ways to access self-confidence rather than becoming a cult follower and parroting trainers' words.

I kept walking.

Once he had a good hold on me, he leaned in pulling me close saying, "Stay, you'd make a great teacher. Stay, you'll be one of the special ones." It was just more bullshitting to keep me from leaving; to keep him from looking bad. It was surreal.

I was still walking towards the exit.

There were two men at the door and I was afraid they weren't going to let me leave. I used all the logic he'd used at the beginning of the seminar to counter whatever he was saying to try and make me stay. I was trembling inside and scared.

"Sandra, you made a commitment to stay the course."

"You were the one who said in the first teaching you gave that we had to be true to ourselves; to find our own center and our own process. I've decided what you're teaching is not for me."

"But you made a commitment to me and to the group to stay."

Finally, I got free of his arm and walked through the door. Free, thank God, I was free at last.

On the drive back to Virginia Beach I kept trying to figure out what to say to my friend who'd paid for me to attend the seminar, especially after she'd gotten so much help from their processes.

While I was in New York City I met others who'd gone through this process and they either said it was the best thing they'd ever done or it was the worst experience of their life. Strange. Years later, I looked up stories on the internet and they all said the same thing I'd said all those years ago. The same plan, the same formula just with different outcomes.

I need a little something sweet after that story. Luckily, I had lots of zucchini and I love these poppy seed muffins.

Zucchini Lemon Poppy Seed Muffins

2 cups flour

¾ cup sugar

1 ½ teaspoons baking powder

½ teaspoon salt

¾ cup milk

¾ cup vegetable oil

2 eggs

1 ½ cups grated zucchini

2 tablespoons poppy seeds

2 teaspoons grated lemon zest

1 teaspoon vanilla

1. Preheat the oven to 350 degrees.
2. In a large bowl, mix the flour, sugar, baking powder and salt.
3. In another large bowl, mix milk, oil, and eggs. Beat until smooth.
4. Add the zucchini, poppy seeds, lemon and vanilla.
5. Mix in gently with the liquid.
6. In batches, add the dry ingredients to the wet ingredients, mixing thoroughly each time.
7. Line a muffin pan with 12 muffin cups and divide the batter equally among them.
8. Bake at 350 degrees until a toothpick inserted into the center comes out clean—about 20 minutes.

Serve.

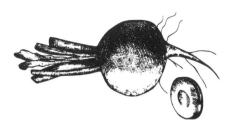

Literary Agent
Summer Borscht

You might be wondering how I became a literary agent. Well, I was living in Virginia Beach with my accountant sister, Brenda. It was summer and I was taking care of her nine year old son, Colin, whom I adored. I'd recently gotten a divorce. Another divorce. *The Sandra Martin Show*, a half hour weekly program I hosted aired on local television. I interviewed New Age speakers (Native Americans, dream interpreters, Edgar Cayce experts and many others) and it was on hiatus. I had also been working for the local PBS station. I had tried to make a major move to national PBS by producing a similar series and it'd fallen through. I was nursing my wounds, taking it easy and wondering what my next (ad)venture would be. I'd already crashed in a small plane in the Grand Canyon and been lost sailing in the Bermuda Triangle. My life was never boring.

One hot, humid August Tuesday morning the doorbell rang. I opened the door; a young woman was standing there just barely holding back tears. I knew her face but not her name.

She said, "Carol told me you could help me."

"Do what?" I asked.

She came in and sat down on the sofa. I put a box of tissues by her side and she told me her name, which was Norma and then she shared her sad lament. She had a manuscript of cat stories for which she had gotten a big New York publishing contract and a $7,000 promised advance. She needed that money for the IRS. Her New York editor had called her that morning, only an hour ago, crying, and said that the publisher had come in and fired everyone in her department, closed the imprint and her contract was null and void. And to top it all, she said, her editor was eight months pregnant.

"How could that mean publisher be so evil?" She really started crying then.

"Why did Carol think I could help you? I know nothing about publishing." Carol was psychologist, a therapist. What on earth could have compelled her to send this woman to me?

"She said you were the only person she could think of that knew how to deal with big companies." I'd been an award-winning account executive with the PBS station.

"Yes, I do work with big companies but that doesn't mean I'd know what to do about your problem."

Yikes. She was crying again. Really crying. So, I went into the kitchen to make us some jasmine tea and think things through; to give her time to get herself together and give me time to "make up something." On a yellow legal pad, I wrote down the only things I thought would be helpful and it was what I'd do if I was in the same situation. That is a situation where I knew nothing about anything, but that'd never stopped me before. I wrote: 1) if you've sold it once I'm sure you could sell it again; 2) if big companies think you want something back, sometimes it makes them want it too, just in case you know something they don't; 3) and if they aren't interested they can take forever to make a move; 4) I'd write them asking them to return my rights immediately so; 5) I could move on.

Norma took the yellow pad, read my list, took the tissues and left. She didn't say much. I hoped I helped but made a mental note to tell Carol to stop sending people my way. This had happened before.

Norma returned that afternoon all bubbly, sweet and upbeat. "I'd like you to read my letter."

"OK."

Her letter requested her rights back in a very professional, almost lawyerly way. It sounded great until the last paragraph which said; if you have any problems, please call Sandra Martin at 804 422 4921.

"Wait, wait, Norma, you can't say that. I know nothing about this business."

"Oh dear."

The bubbly smile started to disappear and she began sobbing again. I said soothing things, quietly walking her to the front door. Just leave my name in; I'm sure it'll be alright.

Damn, I really do have to call Carol.

About two weeks later my phone rang early one morning. A man, with a high squeaky voice shrieked into my ear: "I don't know who you are, I've never heard of you. You have no right to do this. We have a contract."

And he went on and on. I couldn't get a word in edgewise to ask what the heck this was about. I'm trying to think who I could've upset so much. I haven't been doing *anything* plus I'm generally an easy going, mild mannered southern lady. Finally, he says her name, Norma, and I realize that this must be the "evil" publishing company. No wonder she was so upset. He was obnoxious. By then, I had become upset for both of us. I assumed my most steely southern magnolia personality, "In all my years of doing business I've never had anyone speak to me in this tone of voice. Because of your attitude and your abominable behavior, you are going to have to renegotiate this entire deal." Simultaneously an entirely different part of my brain was saying to me in a loud, almost screaming, inner voice, Sandra what the heck are you saying?

But anger had taken over. He says he'll see about that. And I say fine.

We hung up. Loudly.

I walked around cooling off and thinking, damn, he wanted her book. Why didn't I just give him Norma's number, after I found it, of course. While I was looking for her number, he called back, calm and quiet this time and said, "I talked with my publisher and she said we will renegotiate this publishing contract."

I called Norma to give her this jerk's, well Matt's name and number and she says, "Sandra can't you help me? Please. Please. Couldn't you just talk with him? Those guys in New York are so evil." She definitely had a strong belief that publishing or publishers were evil. His negative, belittling attitude had been like a red flag to me. I loved fighting evil! Standing up for the little man or in this case, the little woman was one of my best traits.

Well, I wasn't really busy and it was a big challenge. He had really pissed me off. I went out that afternoon; purchased a paperback book, *How to be Your Own Literary Agent*, read it that night. The next morning I called Matt (the editor) to let him know he'd be dealing with me. I told him exactly what had happened; that I was doing this as a favor for a friend who had been treated badly by his company. And, I added, that I had no experience in the publishing business whatsoever, but nevertheless he'd have to deal with me.

After a few weeks her original $7,000 advance had been negotiated into a $45,000 advance. Matt sent me roses and a card that said, "You should really make this your profession."

I'd found my purpose in life. I'd loved reading since childhood; we were a family of readers. Books were my best friends. Books had influenced every aspect of my life—from my mentor, Dr. George Ritchie's *Ordered to Return*; *My Life After Dying* to *There is a River* by Tom Sugrue to *The Way of the White Clouds* by Lama Govinda. These books had informed my life and understanding how the world, both inner and outer worlds really worked. Books helped me through all those down, negative periods as well as moving me into the next phase of my life.

From that small favor, helping Norma, I realized that becoming a literary agent was what I was meant to do. My goal was to bring this entire genre, the mind/body/spirit as well as the paranormal/deep spirituality to the masses. I could see that people were searching for understanding as to why they were here, what was life all about, and looking for answers to life's deepest questions.

I cold-called publishers in New York City and asked the names of editors that were interested in what was then called, New Age Books, (there were only four or five) got their names, made appointments, drove my little car to Manhattan, slept on a friend's sofa and talked to every editor who'd see me. I loved discovering new authors, reading manuscripts, and helping those manuscripts be born as a hardback mainstream book; it was my raison d'etre.

For a while, I worked with a big literary agency in New York, but found out that they never did what they said they'd do. And never paid me a penny from the five books I sold through them. I struck out on my own.

That is how I became a literary agent.

I think Borscht is a perfect complement to that story. There was a place on the Lower Eastside, a Polish restaurant I think, that served this delicious soup.

Summer Borscht

5 medium fresh beets (about 2 pounds)
Sea salt
2 cups chicken or vegetable stock
16 oz sour cream plus extra for serving
¼ cup sugar
2 tablespoons fresh lemon juice
2 teaspoons white vinegar
2 teaspoons salt
2 teaspoons black pepper
2 cups English cucumbers, seeds removed and diced
½ chopped scallions, white and some of the green parts
2 tablespoons chopped fresh dill plus extra for serving

1. Peel the beets. Drop into a pot of boiling salted water and cook until tender, about 30–40 minutes. Remove the beets, setting aside 2 cups of the cooking liquid for the soup.
2. In a large bowl mix together 2 cups of the beet liquid, the chicken stock, sour cream, yogurt, sugar, lemon juice, vinegar and the salt and pepper. Cut the beets into slices or chunks; add them to the soup, along with the cucumber, scallions and dill.
3. Cover with plastic wrap and chill for at least 4 hours or overnight.
4. Season to taste and serve cold with a dollop of sour cream and a sprig of dill.

Serves 4 to 6.

Dream Synchronicity
Flounder with Capers

It was the mid-80s and I had made my decision to be a literary agent after working for WHRO-TV. I drove to Manhattan from Virginia Beach, across the Chesapeake Bay Bridge, straight up Route 13 to Delaware, then across the Delaware Bridge to the New Jersey Turnpike. I did this every few weeks to have face-to-face meetings with editors. I knew one person in Manhattan and slept in her six year old son's bed while he slept on the sofa. The sheets had cartoon figures on them and the ceiling had airplanes hanging from it. Sweet.

Almost immediately, everyone I met seemed to think I should move to NYC. I always said the same thing: New York is dirty, the people rude. I live where I can see the sun come up every morning, walk on the beach and live around people who are on the same "new agey" wave-length as me. No, thank you. In January I turned my chosen location into a marketing piece. I sent a photograph of myself sitting on the beach, in January, reading a manuscript with a cover that said, "Your next bestseller" to various editors and acquaintances I'd met.

In November of that previous year, I had a dream. In the dream I was standing in the doorway of a small studio apartment and a young man was speaking very quickly to me, as if I was about to run away and he had to talk fast. As he walked around the small space, he said, "This is my apartment; I'm going to LA to edit a film for Turner TV. I'll be gone for six months. I know nature is important to you and there is a courtyard outside."

Interrupting I say, "Excuse me, but all I see is a brick wall outside that window."

He says, "Well, if you lean out the kitchen window you can see a tree down in the courtyard."

As I awoke, I heard the words: Seventh Avenue in the 50s.

I told my sister Brenda about this dream as we were driving to our parents for Thanksgiving. Brenda is a finance person and not given much to dream interpretation but said with supreme confidence, "I know exactly what that dream means–you are to go back into television and make small projects. He was a TV person, the apartment was small. It was a simple, straightforward message." And she continued: "This literary agent stuff is too hard." That was certainly true.

It made good interpretative sense to me: small apartment, small projects, Turner was television. After accepting her interpretation, the dream went out of my mind.

Cut to mid-February. My sister and I were watching TV late one night when the phone rang. It was very late, like around midnight. I said hello. A young man responded, not with hello, but, "I understand you are looking for an apartment to sublet in NYC."

"No," I replied, with a little edge to my voice. "I am not looking for an apartment in New York City; you must have the wrong number."

Not deterred, a very New York characteristic as I was quickly learning, the young man continued, "I am going to LA to edit a film for Turner Broadcasting and I'll be gone for six months and I want to sublet my apartment. The price is $900 a month." Judith, he reported, had given him my name. He reiterated, she said you were definitely looking for a sublet. After a brief discussion, during which I assured him that I didn't know anyone named Judith, I told him again, no, I definitely did not want to move to New York City.

I walked back into the living room and Brenda asks, "Who was that calling so late?"

I told her about the curious call. She said, "Gosh, Sandra, don't you remember your dream?

"What dream?" says I.

I've been writing down my life and my dreams in journals since the late 1960s. We immediately went for my dream journal. We read it. The dream was a duplicate of the conversation I'd just had. I was stunned.

I spent the next two weeks thinking about how hardheaded I am. Everyone in the world was telling me to move to New York but I decided I was not interested, mostly for reasons of comfort. I thought about the convoluted, intricate web of connections that God, Universal Spirit, or my higher self had taken just so I could finally get the message. Heavens. First, I had to have this amazing, unbelievably awesome precognitive dream and, importantly, write it down; then I had to tell Brenda the dream and Brenda had to remember the dream. How the message that I was looking for a sublet, even though I wasn't, had gotten to the caller, I had absolutely no idea. Especially since I hadn't told anyone in New York City that I wanted to move there, in fact I'd told them the opposite. I didn't take his number or remember his name, so I was out of luck there. I made the decision then and there to look for an apartment the next time I was in Manhattan.

Near the end of February, I received another late night call from the same young man. "Ms. Martin, I am moving to LA next week and I have not been able to find someone to sublet the apartment. Are you sure you don't want to move here? I've lowered the price to $600?"

The next week I was living on 57th Street in Manhattan. In dreamland speak, Seventh Avenue in the 50s can be translated into 57th Street, I think.

Of course, these are the kinds of events that made me value dreams so much. Over the years, while I worked at the PBS station, I'd researched and written an eight-hour documentary series on dreams. I'd pitched it everywhere but unfortunately had not been able to generate interest from a single television executive. Let me clarify: I got no interest in producing the series from the executives, but lots of interest in dreams. Often after my meetings, I'd be asked questions about their own personal dreams—what they meant, why they had some over and over, others that were just weird, and some that were obviously past life memories. They seemed especially concerned about their children's nightmares and did I know how to deal with those. I continued to work on the dream series. I believed in it.

There was a great French restaurant on 57th Street between Eighth and Ninth Avenues. It was a family restaurant: the son was a documentary producer when he wasn't making drinks and waiting on tables. The father held fort at the front door and the mother took food orders. Each year they traveled back to France for the month of August. The food was glorious. And this is my version of one of my favorite dishes at that restaurant, now sadly closed. I hope they retired and went home to France.

Flounder in Lemon Sauce

2 teaspoons capers, preferably salt-packed

4 flounder pieces 6 to 8 oz.

Salt and pepper to taste

2 tablespoons unsalted butter

1 tablespoon olive oil

2 shallots or green onions, minced

1 garlic clove, minced

$^2/_3$ cup dry white wine

2 tablespoons fresh lemon juice

2 tablespoon chopped fresh flat-leaf parsley

Grated zest of 1 lemon

1. Run water over the capers to wash away some of the salt.
2. Season the fish lightly with salt and pepper.
3. In a large fry pan over medium heat, melt the butter with the olive oil. Cook fish until browned on both sides-6 to 8 minutes total. Take the fish out, set aside.
4. Add the spring/green onions and garlic to the pan and cook, about 2 minutes. Add the wine and lemon juice, increase the heat to medium-high and boil until the sauce thickens slightly, 2 to 3 minutes. Stir in the parsley, capers and lemon zest, and season with salt and pepper.
5. Pour the warm sauce over the fish and serve immediately.

Serves 4.

Peruvian Shaman

Roasted Vegetables
with Eggplant

I was deep into my literary world and enjoying my clients and always on the look-out for new ones. On September 28, 1988, my good friend Kathy and I flew from Norfolk to Wichita Kansas, where Kathy's brother, George, picked us up in his private plane and flew us to the family ranch in Oklahoma. We had dinner at the Stage Coach Inn and I had chicken fried steak for the first time and it was delicious. A rancher and oilman, her brother regaled us with stories of Russia and his recent travels there. He was definitely the big dog in a small town. After rounding up all the keys to the Colorado Springs mountain cabin and the car, a very old Lincoln in pristine condition, Kathy and I were off. I just loved those wide open, flat plains. The light was phenomenal. We spent our first night in Lamar, Colorado.

Kathy was a local A.R.E. follower and had moved to Virginia Beach many years ago from Oklahoma. She was beautiful, eccentric, extremely smart, a heavy smoker and an oil heiress. I agreed to accompany her to close up her mother's mountain cabin. Her mother had died about six months earlier. They were not close. At all.

Kathy was driving, smoking and talking about how much she and her mother disliked each other. How much they fought. How much she worked to destroy everything that Kathy tried to do. Kathy ended with, "Her birthday is coming up soon."

"Oh, yeah," I said, "Mine is too. When is your Mom's?"

"October 30th. When's yours?"

A long silence ensued. October 30th was my birthday, too. I didn't really know what to say since she'd just enumerated all the flaws in her Mom's personality. Some of them I recognized as my own. I looked out the window at the wide open land so different from Virginia.

Kathy kept looking over at me and finally said, "Sandra, are you okay?"

"My birthday is October 30th."

Kathy was such a fine woman that she said "God must've sent you to me to show me that Scorpios can be good people, too."

I breathed a sigh of relief.

I already had two clients in Colorado. Mother Tessa Belieki, a sort of a New Age nun with a monastery and retreat center in Crestone, Colorado. I'd sold her manuscript, *Teresa of Avila: Ecstasy and Common Sense*, a biography of St. Teresa. She'd written a portrait that was touching, uplifting, terribly human and told in a contemporary voice. It was a powerful book.

The other client I wanted to meet was Mary Summer Rain. Mary was an emotionally evocative writer, with a contemporary message conveyed through the eyes and voice of the past.

Colorado was full of paranormal researchers and consciousness speakers from the New Age genre and I wanted to meet as many as I could.

Kathy's family cabin was right out of central casting, all wood paneling, and views of distant mountains with a musical river running nearby. For the first few days we re-visited all her old haunts: bars, old friends, restaurants and shops. It was very nice and laid back.

Finally, we were off to Crestone to see Mother Tessa. Crestone is the highest valley in the United States. We circled mountains, plowed on through many switchbacks, the old Lincoln straining up mountain passes until we finally crested the tallest mountain and looked down onto the most ethereal valley imaginable. Fir trees, juxtaposed with huge sand dunes, the sky so clear blue it was surreal. We arrived at Mother Tessa's Spiritual Life Institute around 2 PM.

Mother Tessa is truly the mother of all she surveys. She was also blond, blue eyed, young and beautiful.

Mother Tessa took us on a tour of the Baca Grande Ranch. It was so clear and we were so high up that we could see mountains 50 miles across to the west and mountains 75 miles to the south to New Mexico. She said the valley was the largest, the size of Delaware, and highest livable valley in the United States. The little town of Crestone was home to the Baca Grande Center, a non-profit organization devoted to world religions. The Baca Grande had temples, churches and centers of many of the world religions. That afternoon we visited a Hindu Temple, a Zen Center, several Tibetan Buddhist centers and ended back at Tessa's Carmelite Monastery. Each spiritual center had a main building surrounded by tiny homes for staff and guests. This extraordinary place was the brainchild of Hanne (and Maurice) Strong and Tessa strongly urged me to visit her while I was in Colorado.

Tessa's personal hermitage was tiny, quaint, cute and cozy. It was a mountain chalet in miniature. At the main center we had dinner and a young man writing a paper on the Carmelites for his anthropology class at Colorado State entertained us with his research. We left, feeling uplifted and enlightened. We drove back down the mountain.

The following day we met Mary Summer Rain. Mary was petite and dark. She had intense, mysterious dark eyes. A woman of gravitas.

Mary Summer Rain was given the name Summer Rain by a blind Chippewa medicine woman, No-Eyes. After many disappointments in life and feeling lost and alone, Mary had cried out for help while meditating alone in the forests of Colorado. As she was sobbing she sensed a presence, looked up and saw No-Eyes. This began a long teacher-student relationship interweaving ancient wisdom, native stories and a new-old philosophy about what we are doing to Mother Earth and how to heal the Mother and ourselves. Her five books are about her relationship with No-Eyes and her friend, Brian Mary Hearts.

The next morning I got in touch with Hanne, developer of Baca Grande and after a long conversation, she said to come on up. She said she had a Peruvian Shaman and a Tibetan doctor there and wanted me to meet them.

Tessa had given me an article to read about the Baca Grande which I read to Kathy as we drove back up the mountain. Basically, the article explained that, in the 1970s, Maurice and Hanne Strong purchased 10,000 acres of the Baca Grande. It was generally known that for thousands of years the land had been used as a place for ceremonies and spiritual healing. In keeping with this tradition, about 1,000 acres were initially separated and given to the Carmelites for Nada Hermitage; The Aspen Institute; Lindesfarne, Mountain Zen Center and Karma Thegsum Tashi Gomang Tibetan Project, Haidakhandi Universal Ashram and other spiritual centers followed.

The article continued: Baca was to be a place of retreat; where seekers could reach awareness with the guidance of great masters; a place where wisdom traditions of the world could be preserved; a setting for interfaith dialogue and engagement; and a unique opportunity to live in harmony with nature by establishing and teaching sustainable living practices.

That sounded good to Kathy and me.

Hanne, a bright blond, with flashing blue eyes met us at the door in a flowing red dress and cowboy boots. Hanne was a very down to earth Danish woman in control of the universe, her own Universe of the Baca Grande Ranch. She was abrupt and harsh with everyone but otherwise fine. It seemed to be her normal mode.

She sent Kathy and me up to Lindesfarne Chapel, and it was soul awakening. Spirituality just leaps from the rocks. The Chapel is built right into the side of the mountain with a yurt-like look to it. Gizala, a German woman ran Lindisfarne. We also met with an extraordinary Tibetan doctor. His energy was charismatic, warm and loving. We walked back down the hill to Hanne's in a cocoon of love.

Mark, who'd sponsored Emilio, the Shaman from Peru, greeted us as we arrived back at Hanne's home. He said that Emilio was resting now but told the story about how Emilio became a shaman (which I did not write down in my journal) and said that Emilio would explain what all the important symbols of his Shamanic practice meant—snake, jaguar, owl, at the ceremonial site and that it was an all night event.

Kathy had decided not to participate, then—changed her mind and said yes. Hanne fixed us a meal that we couldn't eat. No chicken fried steak. It was very strange food-seaweed and unidentifiable brown stuff. Our fellow travelers had dribbled in and finally, we were all assembled. At 9:30 we piled in to Hanne's two four-wheel-drive vans fully-stocked with blankets and trash bags. We provided the courage. And we were off. There were twelve of us. This process was to last from 10 until 6 AM. First it rained. Poured. In the high desert country. Then it cleared off and the stars came out. The clouds rolled back in again. And then it cleared for good. It was an astounding night sky, filled from horizon to horizon, with a zillion stars. By then it was midnight.

Emilio, the Shaman was the image of wisdom personified: intense eyes, long black hair, heavily lined, dark brown face that was Asian looking. He was exotically primitive and he smoked big fat hand-rolled cigars, continuously. He had an old beat-up peaked hat, a beautiful multi-colored woven South American coat over his shoulders and heavy boots.

Kathy had decided, again, not to participate. The driver took her back down the mountain to Hanne's home. So it was just me and eleven strangers.

It was cold, dark, damp and we were told to make a big circle sitting about twelve inches apart and focus in silence and meditation while our Shaman created the right conditions for the spirits. While he was chanting and whistling, he placed various totems or symbols on an elaborately designed blanket. He'd pick up an object, hold it up to the sky, then bow to the four directions, while he talked about the meaning of this totem. We understood nothing of what he said, but the energy was penetrating and, for me, tense. Emilio chanted, sang, whistled (and he was a damn good whistler, too) and prayed for the energy of all the healers to come. The entire ceremony was conducted in Spanish and most of us couldn't understand a word. He'd sing-song talk and whistle for about ten or fifteen minutes while holding up each stone symbol—a jaguar or a snake—then pray to the four directions for each symbol and cover it in smoke. He did this for each of the many symbols spread out on his blanket. In explanation, his very young translator would simply say "He is praying for all the healers to come." Nothing more. Of course, I'd wanted to know exactly what he was saying. He was so sincere and his dedication pulled me in. Unfortunately, his translator's cursory translation pushed me away again.

Sitting there on the cold, damp ground, I cast around for support: a familiar face—something. Almost everyone was from Colorado Springs or Boulder and they looked like regular business people. I wondered what could've brought them out to this midnight gathering of spirits.

At last I caught the eye of Tim, an approachable guy, clean cut, well dressed—a psychologist from Boulder. I moved over near him. I whispered that this was my first time and I didn't know what to expect and was a little scared. What was going to happen to me? He gave me the lowdown on drugs, what to do and what not to do. Mostly it was about "go with the flow" and "don't hold on to the negative." Tim added that he had two children and loved being a father and this was the first time in years he'd done drugs. He seemed anxious, nervous and apprehensive—whispering to me how excited he was and about what he hoped would be a breakthrough for him.

After many, many prayerful ceremonies, we were asked to stand. Emilio brought around a dish with a spout on it and the translator said to sniff from it. Emilio held it up to my nose and turned it up and it just poured right down into my nasal passage. Not really a "sniff." It was a cold, weird sensation and I didn't like it, but it sure cleared my sinuses. We all *sniffed* a combination of what the translator told us was tobacco juice and herbs. As he moved down the line, people started to mill around, breaking out of our perfect circle chatting with one another and smoking pot and cigarettes.

Then Emilio came around again, after much praying and offerings to the spirits, this time with a wine bottle that was repurposed for mescaline. Another round of prayers and offerings and then another round of the wine bottle. It didn't taste bad, sharp and savage flavor. It was like nothing I'd ever tasted before. I had noticed that Emilio had been drinking from that bottle the entire time we'd been there.

I had the first dose and then another. I was ready. I was expecting to be transformed, to see lights and have experiences. But nothing happened. Nothing at all was happening to me. After a while we had another round. Again, nothing happened. I scoured my conscious mind, my super conscious mind and even looked deep in the subconscious, but I found nothing. I was dizzy. That's all. My new friend Tim asked me if I could see the horses galloping across the sky. I looked but saw nothing. Most people were obviously having a fabulous experience. So I sat.

Finally the young interpreter comes over to me and asks, "Are you okay?" I am the only one still sitting in the circle while the others have wandered off. They seem to be in deep conversation with another world. I tell him, I'm fine but I am not having any "experiences."

He goes over to Emilio and they confer. Emilio walks towards me, looking at me intently, studying my energy. He looked around me, above me and he and the interpreter talk for a while. There is a great deal of back and forth, almost arguing, with serious faces.

Finally, Emilio took his feathers and brushed my aura. He whistled around my head. All the time, he and his protégé are conferring. He obviously asked the interpreter to run and get his pipe because he does just that. Emilio took big puffs of smoke and blew it around my body. They talk again. The interpreter asks me if I meditate; do I have a spiritual practice? They are looking at me intently. I have been meditating since I was about 17, I tell them. After a bit more discussion, the interpreter turned to me and said, "The medicine acts on the blockages in your chakra system and you don't seem to have any blockages so you can go back to the ranch if you like." Then they turned their backs and walked away. They left me standing there in the high desert at 3 AM with an intense headache; I was cold to the bone, extremely disappointed and tired.

I realized then all that meditating for so many years had paid good dividends. But honestly, I was looking for an extraordinary mind-bending experience. Drugs were not for me, apparently.

I walked back down the road to the van, and got inside. Sleep is impossible. Eventually the group finished and our two vans drove back to Hanne's just as the sun was coming up. I was exhausted, had a severe headache and wish I'd stayed at the Tibetan Center. That Tibetan doctor was the sweetest, nicest man.

Kathy drove us back down the mountain and when we got back to her Mom's cottage, I went to bed. By then it was 2 in the afternoon and I slept until 7:30 that night. While sleeping I dreamed I was picking out jewels, great big emeralds, rubies, sapphires and perfect diamonds. I thought that was a good dream with great symbols.

That trip was exploratory in oh-so-many ways. I met with many extraordinary paranormal researchers and self-help lecturers in the field. One was Adam Trombly. Adam was an inventor and, at that time, the Director of Project Earth for the Institute of Advanced Studies in Aspen. He patented the "Closed Path Homopolar Generator," which was an energy generator. He told us about the ozone depletion, the oxygen depletion, multinationals and what the FBI did to him after a Russian KGB Agent tried to buy his generator from him and about how his father was killed by the Derrick Incident in Maryland and how funny he thought it was that George Washington cultivated hemp. Most of all he laughed and laughed.

The visit ended and Kathy and I were filled with sort of a sad joy. I told Kathy, as Kahlil Gibran says, he loves overmuch. He was truly a genius.

We took a plane home to Virginia Beach soon after. And a day later I was in my car driving to Manhattan to my little sublet and to talk with editors.

Every travel adventure brings me back to my favorite meals. We ate lots of meat while we were out West and now it was back to veggie-town.

Roasted Vegetables

2 eggplants cut into ½ inch pieces

6 tomatoes, seeded and cut into ½ inch pieces

4 yellow squash, cut into ½ inch pieces

2 onions, quartered

3 cloves garlic, chopped

Mixed herbs to taste, basil, parsley rosemary and sage

Olive oil to taste

Salt and pepper to taste

1. Preheat oven to 400 degrees.
2. In a large bowl, mix pieces of eggplant, tomatoes, squash, onions and garlic.
3. Toss with the herbs and moisten all with the olive oil.
4. Salt and pepper to your taste.
5. Spread across a baking sheet and roast at 400 degrees or until tender, about 15 minutes.

Serves 4.

Dream of Moving Again
Old Fashioned Soup

After living in my 57th Street sublet for six months, I started to move around quite a bit, here and there and nowhere until I finally landed another sublet on 92nd Street on the Westside. I was there for two years. Clearly I needed a stable place to live. I was praying for a permanent apartment that would be large enough and good for entertaining; of course with extraordinary views—all the things that New Yorkers yearn for. In the meantime I was sleeping at my office. It seemed lots of the tenants had made their offices homes, too. The building had been an apartment building before converting to business, so it was easy to do.

For months I'd been looking for a place to move that was close to work. By now I was working extremely long hours. I definitely didn't want more of the Upper Westside. I was tired of dodging stroller babies on the sidewalks and crying children in every restaurant. I looked and looked but found nothing I liked or that "spoke to me."

Wrong. Actually, I had found one place near the office that was perfect; it was newly renovated, had large rooms and it was right off of 7th Avenue only four blocks from the office (funny, I just "heard that" Seventh Avenue in the 50s from my first

moving dream). It just didn't work out for reasons I didn't understand for years. Someone later told me that the rental agents, two
rough-looking although very quiet mafia types, expected big cash
bribes to agree to a contract. I had no context for bribing agents,
so I kept looking.

Apartment hunting in New York City was almost a full time
job. The apartments go fast, the prices are steep and you don't get
much for your money. Finally, I gave up and just stopped looking
altogether.

One night, weeks after I'd stopped looking, I dreamed that
I was being shown an apartment by my realtor. We met on 57th
Street and walked into a long and spacious lobby. There was beautiful artwork all the way down the wall to the elevators. We took
the elevator up and walked down a hallway. When he unlocked
the door and motioned for me to walk inside, there sat my mother's mother. She was alone in the middle of the room perched on a
small chair. She looked up at me and just smiled. I looked around
and knew this was the apartment I was looking for. My mother's
mother was dead. But there she was, as sweet as could be, smiling
and holding the space for me.

For two weeks Lisa and I walked up and down 57th Street
and all the streets in between looking for that lobby. We never
could find it. Finally I gave up.

More weeks passed and I got a call from my realtor. He thinks
he's found an apartment I might like. Hurry because it'll go in
hours. I grab my coat and walk up to meet him at 57th and Broadway and we walk down to 347 W. 57th Street. The lobby is huge,
long and artwork all along the left side. I am holding my breath,
anxious, but eager to see the apartment. We take the elevator up
and he unlocks the door to 35A and as he opens it, I see that it is
the same apartment as the one I'd dreamed about.

I say to him, "I'll take it," and he says, "No! Really! Sandra,
you have to look at it first."

"Nope," I say, "I know it is the one."

And it was. I lived there for the next 10 years. Fifty-Seventh

Street was my street. I loved that apartment. I could see Central Park, the Hudson River, north to south, the World Trade Center and everything in between. It was a beautiful place. And in it, I cooked for everyone. We had FIONS (Friends of the Institute of Noetic Sciences) fundraiser dinners. One was for astronaut Edgar Mitchell, founder of IONS. I made dinners for Dean Radin, Colin Wilson, Richard Belzer and many others. I had parties for author's book debuts. Many clients slept on my sofa and it was just perfect. In fact, in all my life of living here and there, it is still my favorite home.

A young man who worked for me, Lars, loved my soup. He was Swedish, a television documentary producer and all around "I can do anything" kind of guy. If I even hinted that I was making soup for the weekend, he'd be knocking at my door.

Old Fashioned Soup

$^1/_2$ of a chicken or separate legs, thighs and breast
   quarter

Fresh herbs—parsley, thyme, rosemary chopped or you
   can use dried

1 large onion, chopped

$^1/_2$ cup of celery

2 cups diced potatoes with or without skin

2 cups sliced carrots

2 cups butter beans or green peas (frozen is fine)

1 cup $^1/_2$ inch pieces of green beans

Add 1 cup yellow corn (frozen is fine)

Salt and pepper

1. In a big soup pot, add two quarts of water and put in chicken, onion and celery and herbs. Bring to a boil, lower temperature after boiling point and maintain a simmer for 20/30 minutes.
2. After it has simmered and the meat has started to fall off the bones, move the pot off the stove and let it cool.
3. After it has cooled a bit, strain the liquid, saving it.
4. Pull all the meat off the bones, shredding the chicken as you go.
5. Put the liquid back in the pot.
6. Add the vegetables and the shredded chicken, except for the corn.
7. Simmer for 30 to 35 minutes till vegetables are soft and flavors melded.
8. Add the corn just before the soup is done.
9. Salt and pepper to taste
10. This is an Italian tip that Marcella Hazan introduced to the US and I often include it in my soups. An inch of parmesan cheese rind added in with the vegetables.
11. At the end of cooking and just before serving, I take two tablespoons of butter and swirl it around in the soup.

Serves six.

New York City
Paul's Pasta Fagioli Soup

In New York City you don't necessarily eat out because you're hungry. Eating out in New York City is "the thing to do, see and be seen: eating out is an adventure." As a literary agent, I dined out often, almost always for lunch and at least twice a week for dinner. It was nicer discussing business over dinner and a fine wine with editors or clients.

My office was at 52nd and Broadway and one of my favorite restaurants, Da Tommaso's was just around the corner on 8th Avenue. Claudia Trivelas was Italian with lots of dark curly hair, perfect skin and many, not just me, believed she should've been a hand model because she had perfect hands. She was an extremely close friend from the moment I met her. She'd offered me her son's bed—the one with cartoons on the sheets—whenever I drove in from Virginia Beach. On multiple occasions she also rescued my car from being towed for parking in a no-parking zone. She gave me helpful hints about what to do and not to do in Manhattan. She was a life-saver in so many ways.

Claudia was also a perceptive and dedicated astrologer. She always gave me great advice.

We would have dinner at Da Tommaso's almost every Friday night, especially while I was agonizing through a really bad obsessive (on my part) relationship. She worked at MTV, which was nearby and we'd meet at Da Tommaso's. It was a standing appointment; Friday night at 7:30, give or take, depending on how late we were working.

Da Tommaso's is an old time Italian restaurant: small dining room, a tiny bar and overseen by a smooth, handsome and very smart maître d' named Paul.

We'd been meeting on Friday nights for weeks and the restaurant was busy but never crowded. Then, a tiny two line item in the local gossip column about a movie star being seen there having dinner on a Friday night changed everything. The next Friday night there was a long line to get in. We were happy for Da Tommaso's but unhappy we'd have to stand in line. But we stood on the cold New York City sidewalks and waited. We loved Da Tommaso's food.

After a bit Paul came outside and walked up and down the line. He saw us and motioned for us to follow him. We did and were seated quickly. I thanked him and then asked him why he did that. He said, "After the item in the newspaper we've been packed but trends come and go and I always want to take care of my regular customers first." He was always gracious and savvy.

The food was excellent and I would often have Pasta E Fagioli, a bean and pasta soup. It was the perfect soup for cold winter nights in Manhattan.

Since moving back to Bracey I modified the recipe to suit my southern style of cooking. I call it "In Honor of Paul: Pasta Fagioli Soup."

Paul's Pasta Fagioli Soup

2 tablespoons olive oil

1/2 cup each—sliced into 1/4 inch pieces—carrots, celery
and onion.

1 clove garlic, minced

Herbs to taste—a pinch to a handful
(parsley, rosemary, thyme)

Salt and pepper to taste

3 cups chicken stock

1 can Navy beans or Great Northern beans, rinsed

1 cup cooked chicken, roughly chopped

3/4 cup uncooked pasta (either Campanelle—looks like
little cones or Orecchiette—looks like little ears)

1 cup spinach or kale, cleaned and cut into
1/4 inch ribbons

1/3 cup grated Parmesan cheese

1. Put the oil in a large soup pot and heat on high.
2. Add the veggies and garlic, lower the heat and sauté
   until tender
3. Mix in herbs
4. Then add the chicken stock, beans, cooked chicken, and
   pasta. Bring to boil and cook for 20 minutes.
5. In the last 10 minutes, add the spinach or kale ribbons.
6. At the end of cooking, stir in the Parmesan cheese.
7. Pass additional grated cheese for garnish.

Serves four to six.

Romance

Chicken in a Bag

The lovely island of Malta, in the Mediterranean Sea, right below the heel of Italy's boot, was where my sister and her husband had an apartment or flat, as they called it. This was their get-away, a cool down, from the desert sands. They'd moved from California to Saudi Arabia and were working for Aramco, American Arabian Oil Company. Seizing the opportunity, I took a trip to Malta.

My sister was in Saudi so her friend Marie (Marie pronounced Mari) picked me up from the airport. The next thing I knew I was installed in the town of Sliema, in an elegant marble apartment looking out at the Mediterranean Sea. Colorful small boats were docked everywhere; a promenade across the street was crowded with young mothers pushing babies in strollers and lovers with hands entwined. Of course, there was a cool sea breeze and salty sea air. It was beyond perfect.

Marie had a daycare center which kept her super busy. Even so, the next day she agreed to be my tour guide, so to speak, since Malta was so small, it didn't take long to drive around the island. After that quick trip, I was on my own. The bus cost five cents to go anywhere on the island. It seemed everyone on Malta spoke five or six languages so I had no problem with making myself understood, even with my southern accent. Occasionally, I borrowed Marie's VW bus. Five gears. The steering wheel was on the right, and driving was on the "other side" of the street, not the one I was used to driving on. Streets were very narrow; everything was compact.

One day, while trying to find my way to a glass factory showroom, I had an experience that showed me just how small the island was. I had come to a circle with five narrow streets feeding into it. Overwhelmed, I just stopped to let everyone else go. Then I'd decide which of those streets was the correct one that would deliver me to the glass factory. But the other cars stopped, too. There seemed to be lots of conversation between them. Finally, one man gestured out the window and yelled, "Go! Blonde American Woman, Go! Go! Go!" I went. As I said, it was a small island. Word travels.

I toured Valletta and the ancient temples, as well as all the Knights of St. John sites. I often met Marie at the historic Malta Club to have drinks after her daycare closed. She'd meet her friends to play tennis and I'd sit and read. This one special day, Marie and I were again going to the Club as she was meeting a friend for tennis. As we walked in I saw this man standing at the bar. An extremely handsome man. Our eyes met and it was electric.

"Marie, who is that man?"

She said dismissively, "Don't talk to him. He's an Arab."

"Oh. Ok."

We got a table by the window, we talked, ate, her friend came, they left to go and play tennis.

Five minutes later, the man at the bar came over to the table. To this day, I have no idea what he said, what I said, but the upshot was that I agreed to go with him to Cairo the next morning.

Finally, Marie was done with her tennis game and she dropped me off at the apartment. I was getting a little frantic trying to figure out what to do. I knew when I told her that she'd be over-the-top upset. While I was trying to decide when to call her, I was packing my suitcase. For some reason, I didn't think, "Wait a minute, what am I doing?" Nope. I was busy trying to decide what to take with me on the plane. I decided to call her the next morning, right before he was to pick me up.

I called her at 8:30. She was so stunned that she said nothing at all, for which I was grateful. My traveling companion's car came at 9 and we drove to the airport. I wasn't nervous about going off with a complete stranger, but I was hyper alert. He kept asking, what's the matter? Nothing, I'd say. He got our tickets and we sat waiting for the plane. We were walking out on the tarmac to the plane when up screeched Marie in her VW van—right up to the plane. It was a small airport on a small island. She could do that. She jumped out, ran to me, grabbed my arm and was pulling me out of the line. He, meanwhile, carefully held on to my other arm and was keeping me in line. He had a very puzzled look on his face; he had no idea what was going on. Marie said, "Your sister will kill me if I let you go off with this man. You cannot go. You must not go." He meanwhile was saying nothing and neither was I. By now, we had attracted the full attention of everyone at the airport. The line stopped. Officials came to talk to Marie. They spoke in Maltese. I did not understand one word. It was a very intense conversation. They were arguing with Marie. Then, they turned to me and in English asked, "Do you want to go with this man?" I said, "Yes, I do." And we got on the plane. Marie was crying. I said I'd call her that night.

I knew nothing about this man. I was getting on a plane to go to Cairo and I had no other plans. We settled in our seats, the plane took off, we had snacks, we had tea, and still we didn't talk. It is a five hour flight. I was finally getting nervous. Quietly and gently he said, "Put your arm through mine and you'll feel better." I did that and I did feel better. We talked. He was from Alexandria, Egypt and was a medical doctor trained in London. He was head of the Food and Drug Administration for the country of Libya. He seemed like a perfectly nice, normal man and he was.

We arrived in Cairo and, over the next few weeks, I had personal tours of all the ancient sites. We explored the pyramids after normal tourism hours, visited the bazaars and went out into the desert for evening picnics. If I even looked at something he'd buy it for me and one for my daughter, too. Wow, we were in love. I felt like I was drugged. It was immediate, complete, desperate, and overwhelming love. He was introducing me to all his friends. His friends were doctors, engineers, developers, and successful businessmen.

After many dinners and introductions I had stopped really listening to the Arabic conversations that were often interspersed with English for me. It just sounded like music to me until I was meeting his accountant, the man who handled his money. It was a business meeting, not an entertaining Sandra time. In English, I heard my romantic sweetheart say we were going to be married. Something clicked or maybe more appropriately un-clicked in my love and lust induced state. No, no, I was pretty sure I didn't want to get married. Never again.

After three of weeks of being treated like a princess, I actually began to get bored. There was no one to talk with about all those spiritual and metaphysical things I liked to discuss; not one other woman I'd met was interested in these subjects. And my Arab Romeo just couldn't comprehend what I was saying when I talked about all that fascinating information from the psychic Edgar Cayce about the pyramids and Atlantis. He'd ask me with a genuinely puzzled expression; what are you talking about?

The bloom was quickly going off the rose. I was still madly in love but I didn't want to be married, one man's woman, in a world I didn't know. So I told him I wanted to leave. He couldn't believe it. Heck, I could hardly believe I was saying it myself. After much protestation, he got me a ticket to go to Greece and then to Malta. We'd had almost a month of fantasy-romantic-all-encompassing passion. It'd been great; actually beyond great it'd been awesome.

On the plane flying to Athens, it began to sink in that I'd left a man I truly loved. I thought, what am I doing? This man truly loves me and wants to love and adore me and take care of me forever. He was handsome, cosmopolitan, generous, and a very loving person. Those other thoughts about the entire Arab mindset of men and women went out the window.

Love was the thing we all sought, wasn't it? Finding true love is rare and why was I so afraid? When I arrived to my hotel in Athens I decided I'd call him and say I was wrong I wanted to go back to him. But it wasn't meant to be. It seemed that Greece and Egypt were having a spat and weren't speaking so there was no connection: No phone calls allowed.

I toured Greece for a few days then I flew back to Malta. Marie was so grateful that I was alive and safe. But thereafter she kept her eye on me like a hawk!

My handsome lover eventually visited me in the United States and cooked for me and for my friends. He was a great chef. And he loved to serve us dinner. Sometimes I thought he missed his calling. He'd have been a great restaurateur.

Chicken in a Bag

Preparation time: 20 minutes Cooking Time: One hour+

One large chicken—3 to 4 pounds

Juice of one lemon, saving the lemon

1–2 cloves garlic, as needed

Olive oil, as needed

Salt and pepper to taste

Cayenne pepper (optional)

1 cup red potatoes

1 cup green beans

2 small onions, quartered

¼–½ cup small carrots

1 large (28 oz.) can tomatoes

1. Preheat the oven to 350 degrees.
2. The night before, take the chicken, wash it, dry it and rub it with lemon juice, garlic, salt and pepper. Insert the lemon into the chest cavity. Put the rubbed chicken in a large air tight plastic bag and refrigerate overnight.
3. The next morning, take the chicken out, throw away the lemon and rub olive oil over the chicken with more garlic, salt and pepper. And cayenne pepper if you like things spicy.
4. Put the chicken in a cooking bag and inside the bag around the chicken, in little groupings add the vegetables.
5. Over all of that pour a large can of whole tomatoes.
6. Cook 1½ hours until done.

It makes a great meal with rice or pita bread. Serves 8.

Greece

Real Greek Salad

While I was in Greece I visited the museums, walked around the Parthenon trying to get in touch with my inner Athena, went to Delphi hoping for a whisper of inspiration, climbed up some serious mountains and took a bus to see the Temple of Poseidon.

Along the way, I was bothered repeatedly by men and teenage boys who harassed me. I am sure being a young woman, blonde and friendly, marked me as being available. Frankly, it was a horrible experience. I found myself molested daily by Greek men. It was the most terrifying experience I've ever encountered as a woman traveling alone. Even a priest grabbed my breasts while giving a lecture about his church! A woman near me said "Did he do what I just saw him do?" He was so practiced at it—I was so surprised that I said nothing and just slipped out of the church to get away from him. The woman came with me and we talked about the horrors of a woman traveling alone in Greece. She was lucky; she had her husband with her and I hung out with them the rest of my stay. I was eager to get away from Greece and so sad because I had been so excited to go there.

The good thing was that in the States one of my all time favorite things to eat was a Greek Salad. I liked everything about it and in Greece I just ordered a salad; it came Greek.

Recipe: Real Greek Salad

One English cucumber, sliced in 1-inch slices

Two or three large tomatoes cut in quarters

One medium onion, quartered

1 clove minced garlic

Copious amounts of crumbled Feta cheese or 1/4 cup

A handful of Greek olives or 1/4 cup

1/4 to 1/2 cup olive oil

1/4 cup red wine vinegar,

1 tsp. dried Greek oregano

Salt and pepper to taste

1. In a bowl, put the cucumbers, tomatoes, onion and garlic and pile the Feta atop all.
2. In a jar or container with a lid, put the oil, vinegar, oregano, salt and pepper to taste and shake until mixed thoroughly.
3. Pour over all.

Serves 4.

A Final Note

We kept in touch. He visited me in the states, he wrote me romantic poetry, he sent my mother flowers, and he was more than dreamy. But still I couldn't bring myself to marry him.

While I was working in Athens, Georgia at the University of Georgia, he came to visit me. After his arrival and our sweet reunion, the following evening I invited some friends to meet him. They asked all sorts of questions and one was where was he going next.

He stood up, took an airline ticket out of his pocket, the ticket unfolded like an accordion all the way to the floor while telling these good girlfriends of mine that he wanted me to go with him to tour all the Scandinavian countries. For a month. He said that when he was in university he didn't have time to go to those countries and he was curious about them.

I was so surprised that before I thought clearly, I told him, in front of everyone, I couldn't do that because I had a job. He hadn't asked me or told me about his plans. Immediately, two of my friends actually stood up and walked up to him and offered to go in my place! I was floored; he was stunned and his face looked it so one woman said, "Just kidding" but the other woman stood there offering herself to him. I couldn't believe it. I mean, really.

He sat down and it was pretty darned quiet for a while until they left.

He was a great chef and made awesome meals for us while he was visiting. He made us what he called "Chicken in a Bag."

He asked, "Did you have cooking bags here in the US?"

"Yes."

"Do you have fresh herbs?"

"Yes."

He thought we all ate fast food and unhealthy food. He'd ask me "Does everybody eat this fried food?"

"Well, we are in the South and so I'd have to say yes, lots of fried food."

"The doctors here must make a good living."

Another interesting bit was that whenever we'd meet he'd say to me, "Sandra, you've got to tell your president that Gaddafi is a crazy man; he is totally insane."

I'd tell him that, unfortunately I did not have access to my President like he did to his. He was eager to leave his job and Libya.

Many years passed and I was in LA on business and met a producer who was from Egypt via London. She had a photograph of the pyramids prominently displayed on her office wall. We talked about Egypt during our meeting and afterwards she asked if I wanted to drop by her apartment to have a glass of wine and talk more about my interests in the pyramids. She said she missed talking about her homeland.

One afternoon, not long afterwards, I called and we did meet. We talked for hours about the world of the Middle-East, things changing so fast and wondering what was going to happen next.

During the course of the evening I told her about my Handsome Arab Experience. She asked me his name. I told her. She asked me about his history, which I told her. She knew who he was and she told me what had happened to him. He'd gotten away from Gaddafi, away from Libya, had married a nice Swiss woman and was living in Switzerland. They had three daughters and seemed very happy.

He was a good memory I will always have. Maybe we'll meet next lifetime. I hope so.

Phillippa's Indian Curry

Phillippa (with that unusual spelling) was a Brit and was on the Manhattan FIONS Board-Friends of the Institute of Noetic Sciences. The original organization IONS, was founded by Edgar Mitchell, one of the Apollo 14 Astronauts and the sixth man to walk on the Moon. I joined the FIONS Board when I moved to New York City. I represented one of the researchers at IONS and had close relationships with the staff.

At a Board meeting in Phillippa's gorgeous Upper Eastside apartment, she served this delicious curry. I'd never had this cooked by someone I knew-remember I was from the South and Indian food was something I read about. It was so good I asked her for the recipe.

She said, "Oh, I just throw in whatever I have in the refrigerator."

So, this is what she had that day in her refrigerator and this is how I cook it whenever I'm hungry for some Indian food.

Phillippa's Indian Curry

3 tablespoons butter

2 tablespoons of curry

1 onion, sliced

3 cloves garlic

Salt and pepper to taste

2 cups bite-sized cauliflower pieces

2 cups diced potatoes

2 cups sliced or diced carrots

1 pint plain yogurt

1. Melt the butter in the base of a large pot. Add the curry powder and sauté the curry for about three minutes.
2. Add the cauliflower, potatoes, and carrots into the pot and add enough water to cover veggies. Over high heat, bring to a boil. Decrease to medium and simmer the vegetables until soft.
3. Add 1 pt. of plain yogurt to the vegetables once cooked and let simmer for another 15 minutes.
4. Serve over rice.

Serves 6.

Past Life
Chicken with Apricots

When I was young girl growing up on a tobacco farm in southern Virginia, I had dreams in which I was speaking French. After my French dreams I would feel quiet and down-spirited (now I realized I was depressed) for days. Once when I was around 10 or 12, I got up my nerve and tried to tell my Mom that I'd been dreaming in another language but she dismissed the dream and me with a quick, "I don't believe a word of that." She had no context nor did I.

As a child, I also had long and involved dreams of attending classes in an off-planet university. When I had these dreams I would wake up exhausted from night time mental work. Other than that my dreams, except for a lifetime of intense snake dreams, have been pretty normal. My dream life has given me insights into decisions I've made; every relationship I've begun and ended. I've had precognitive dreams ever since I can remember. Dreams have been insightful, funny, and have provided valuable information for everything in my life.

My French dreams lasted from my childhood until I was almost 50. After I was an adult, I assumed they were from remnants of a past life that I was tuning into, for some unknown reason. They were puzzling dreams and finally I just let them go.

Each time I had another one I simply acknowledged it and moved on. They were a part of me and I ceased to puzzle over them.

When I was traveling often people asked me if I wanted to go to Paris. I always said no. When I finally, after many years, looked at my travel footprint, I had unconsciously traveled to almost every country circling France, but had never stepped foot on French soil.

Living in New York City, there were travel deals galore to most major European cities. I traveled, but never opted for France. That was until I represented the comedian and actor Richard Belzer. He was best known as Detective Munch from *Homicide: Life on the Street*. After the series ended, he played Detective Munch on *Law and Order: Special Victims Unit*. Richard and his wife, Harlee, were friends because his brother was married to my good friend Emily. I met Emily when I first moved to NYC and we bonded immediately; both of us were Virginia girls.

Eventually as Richard's literary agent I represented and sold his book, *UFOs, JFK and Elvis: Conspiracies You Don't Have to Be Crazy to Believe*.

Richard and Harlee had a house in France and they were always inviting me to visit. Richard was mesmerized by the conspiracy world and, as I was the doyenne of that world at the time, we became fast friends. It seemed that almost everyone writing a manuscript about a conspiracy eventually made their way to NYC to tell me their story.

Richard had a super sharp mind that remembered every little detail of even the most diverse conspiracies. He was almost a walking encyclopedia. He knew that I knew what was real and what was not. Many conspiracies were just a "look over here; not over there" type of obfuscation promoted by government agencies or their affiliates. Then there were the real ones; the ones that never went away. We'd talk for hours and hours about UFOs, JFK, and another client of mine, Richard's hero, Jim Marrs.

Jim Marrs was a superstar client and one of my best friends in the conspiracy world. Whenever he was in New York, sleeping on my sofa, we'd talk until all hours. He was a fount of nerve-jangling information and sometimes I'd have to say, "Just stop, Jim. I can't take any more."

Jim had written *Crossfire: The Plot That Killed Kennedy* and in paperback it had reached *The New York Times* bestseller list and was the basis for the Oliver Stone film *JFK*. I'd sold Jim's books: *Alien Agenda: Investigating the Extraterrestrial Presence Among Us*; *Rule by Secrecy: The Hidden History That Connects the Trilateral Commissions, the Freemasons, and the Great Pyramids*; and *Psi Spies, The True Story of America's Psychic Warfare Program*.

Jim was truly a superstar.

Emily and Len Belzer (Richard's brother) went to France most summers, while the television series Richard was starring in, *Homicide: Life on the Streets* was on hiatus. I always passed on the invitation even though Emily's reports on the gracious beauty of the countryside, the delicious food, and the wines of France were beyond anything she'd ever experienced. Still I said, no, thank you.

Life in New York City seemed all-consuming. My life as a literary agent was a never-ending job, working long hours at the office, discussions with clients and editors. Because I represented many conspiracy and UFO books I was constantly asking clients, "Where did you read this? Who told you that? How do you know they didn't just now make it up?" As well as making editorial suggestions, I was pitching projects to movie studios, production companies and programmers at various television networks and that only left nights and weekends to read manuscripts. I was tired.

So, that particular summer, when Richard asked if I wanted to fly to France with him, I said yes. Harlee was already there. He said it was a complicated process-from taxi, to plane, to taxi to another airport for another plane, to taxi to a train, to Rodez, the nearest town to where they had their home, and where Harlee would pick us up. We'd fly together. First Class Air France. Luxury all the way.

We arrived and it was all everyone said it'd be. Gorgeous. Harlee had re-modeled an old mill located right on the river, with fields of wildflowers, and orchards. It was a picture book of perfection. The light was enchanting. A magical place for taking long walks.

The subject over each morning's breakfast was, "where shall we have lunch?" Harlee knew all the local cafes. Later, we'd take a slow ride through the lush countryside; stopping for the goats and sheep crossing the road, and the ladies in black with their baguettes. The food was beyond delicious, replete with cheeses that were nothing like the ones in the States, and always accompanied by flavorful wines. We savored those long round-about rides through the countryside talking about life and friends back home and what they were missing. Pretty idyllic.

Okay, the speedy and hyper New York life that I'd left to get some rest was quickly countered by this gentle easy-going pace and it was nice. But after two weeks of *nice* I was bored. As much as I loved everything about their home and our leisurely days, I was getting hyper and nervous. I was feeling unexplainably edgy so after much discussion, Richard and Harlee took me to the airport to fly to Paris. I called Lisa, my daughter and manager of the office, to tell her where I was headed.

I landed at Orly Airport and after getting my luggage and a taxi, headed down the highway to The City of Light, the heart of Paris and to my hotel. Riding along in the quiet, just gazing out the windows and taking it all in, suddenly I was overcome with such a deep sadness that I started sobbing. I was crying so hard I was coughing. The taxi driver handed me tissues but said not a word. I cried all the way to the hotel.

I checked in and called Lisa to say where I was. She gave me the "while you were out" report. In the 24 hours since we'd spoken, she'd run into a friend, who had a friend, who was a parapsychologist in Paris. The Paris friend had called Lisa asking for my hotel and my phone number. Lisa asked if she could share my phone number with her. Sure, I said. I tried not to let Lisa know

I'd been crying, but I knew she was so sensitive to me that she must've known something was wrong.

This intense crying was such a mystery to me that I knew I'd never be able to explain it. We hung up and I lay down on the downy white comforter and started crying again in heavy sobs. After a while, thankfully, I fell asleep. I was perplexed but decided that it must've been something I needed to do-wash away this deep sadness despite not knowing from where the sadness originated. It was so overwhelming that I could not begin to sort it out in my mind and decided to go with it.

It was mid-afternoon and I was awakened by the ringing phone. Thinking it was Lisa, I was confused when a French woman said in English: "Hello, I'm Christine Hardy." I said hello and she spoke as if commanded; "Sandra, you cannot stay in Paris. You cannot. I will come and get you and take you to my country home." And I meekly said okay even though I had no idea who she was. That was strange in itself. No questions—from me!

Not an hour passed when she called from downstairs. I checked out of this nice hotel, after not even sleeping a night there. Soon we were off to her country home by another river-I forget the name of it. It was a two-hour drive, Southwest of Paris.

Christine was, in the French way, beautiful; thick curly dark blond hair with light blond highlights, beautiful blue eyes, slender, quirky, psychic, and smart. She told me she had been married to a parapsychologist who had been studying her psychic ability. They were now divorced. She seemed a little stressed and smoked and drank tea constantly. She had a little contraption that she could plug into her cigarette lighter that heated water. She would squeeze a used tea bag, tossing it out the window and insert a new one in her little pot with a practiced, fluid motion that let me know she'd done this a million times. She kept a small cigarette roller and tobacco papers in her lap while driving and could sift a bit of tobacco onto the paper, roll it up, lick it and light it all done while flying down the highway. I was pretty much in awe. I said nothing.

Throughout the trip I was still crying although without the force of before. Amazingly, she didn't ask me why I was crying. Maybe she knew that I didn't know. The taxi driver from the airport hadn't ask me, either. I just sat crying while she smoked and drank tea and drove. We passed lots of farms on our way to her house and somehow that was soothing to me. I watched tractors plowing fields and dust blowing across the highway as farmers continued their eternal jobs.

When my tears slowed down I was able to ask her why she was so compelled to come and get me; someone she'd never met and had no idea about. She said, "I knew you had to get out of Paris. I had no idea why. I just knew I had to get you quickly out of Paris. I hadn't planned on going to my country house but decided that was the place you needed to be."

I said nothing. It was as if I were in an alternate universe and wasn't sure of my footing.

Her home was a country cottage close to the river and it was soft, easy, and comfortable. Chintz covered sofas and antiques mixed with Plexiglas tables. She was working on a parapsychology paper she said so she'd be busy writing. I could take walks and meditate by the river and everything would be all right. She seemed totally okay now that I was out of the city. Ummm.

She wrote in the mornings. I walked by the river puzzling over my deep sobs while in Paris and wondering why I was not so affected beyond the city limits. Then we would lunch at a little café in town or visit a museum or an old castle for the afternoon, and then make our way back to her house for dinner. After a week I was bored.

I hesitantly said, "I want to go back to Paris."

Christine was confused; "Why do you want to go back when it affects you so badly? And you still don't know why. It could portend something terrible will happen to you. Or something from a past life that is still a big part of your consciousness. Stay here where you are safe."

What she said triggered the memory of a dream I'd had many times, starting in my childhood, of being in Paris. I tell her the dream, which triggers another bout of sobbing:

I am aware that I am dreaming of a past life. I'm walking down a long hallway in a huge building. The walls are made with warm, golden stone blocks and on them are gorgeous tapestries. The stones seem warm and safe to me.

While walking and appreciating the beauty of the building, I am holding a plaque close to my chest. I am aware that I am thinking in French and that I am barely holding tears back. I have long dark hair and am wearing a heavy emerald green dress, with a deeply plunging neckline, and with many jewels around my neck and wrists. The dress is long and drags the floor. I can hear it scraping along. It is the only sound I hear when I am not speaking.

There are people from the nearby village following me down this hallway. It feels as if I am giving them a tour of my home. They are walking a distance behind me, not speaking, not cowering, but obviously cautious.

I am saying to them: "The King built this castle for me. Every tapestry is a work of art."

Inside my soul I am extremely sad but I am also a haughty and arrogant woman. It is as if I am two people in the dream, the watcher and the dreamer. I feel I am not so fond of this life and time period and sense impending doom.

I speak French fluently (naturally) and take pains to point out every detail of the chateau, the home the King built for me, (I seem to keep repeating this in the dream) as well as the grounds. I am especially proud of the beautiful gardens. The gardens gladden my soul for a bit but quickly the sadness comes back.

As I arrive back where we started at the front of the building, (it seems we've walked in a big U and gone outside to the gardens) I say grandly to those following me; "This will be yours now." With a flourish of my skirts, I walk out the door and down three steps. On the wall of the building is the original plaque. Mine is a copy that I am still clutching to my chest. I read it to them.

I tell Christine that whenever I have had this dream, each time I had these "aha moments:" I speak French; that this is a past life and that I can read French. From the dream, I get the impression it wasn't that common for women to be able to read and write. And I was exceptionally proud that I was reading to these people because I knew they couldn't read the plaque. I never remember what the plaque says. It was like it was blanked out of my memory.

Christine carefully writes down my dream as I've told it to her. I've discovered since arriving at her country home, Christine is not only a psychic and parapsychology researcher, she is also a Psychological-Anthropologist with a Ph.D. from Paris University. She conducted cross-cultural investigations into states of consciousness and techniques of mental self-control over a period of several years during her travels in the Middle East, the Far East and Africa. The reason she speaks excellent English is because she worked as a research assistant at Princeton's Psychophysical Research Laboratories (PEAR) for two years in Princeton, New Jersey.

For a long time she says nothing, just looks at me drying my eyes but still crying a little. She writes notes, unfortunately in French, which I can't read outside of my dreams, on her pad. In my mind I'm worrying that she is planning on making me one of her research projects-how strange would that be when I am selling books about parapsychological research. I definitely do not want to be a research subject or have that kind of attention focused on me, for darned sure.

Finally, she speaks solemnly. "I believe you are having a past life dream and you need to process the sadness you didn't get to express during that lifetime. I will drive you back to Paris tomorrow."

I am so relieved. The next morning she says that I can stay with her in Paris, but I say I want to be alone to deal with this and that if she'll just drive, I'll find a hotel. It was a very quiet drive back with not so much smoking or tea drinking. The heaviness in my heart started as soon as we neared the city. We drove up and down a few of the main streets until I saw a hotel sign that said: Cayce. Cayce; spelled just like Edgar Cayce's name, my sign and connection to a safe place. She pulled into the driveway, a big circular entrance, a beautiful hotel and I ran in to see if they had rooms. They did, so I checked in, pulled my bag from Christine's car and told her I'd call her soon.

So far so good. I wasn't even crying when I checked in and felt pretty good.

I called Lisa and told her my new plans, where I was and the things that had been happening to me. I explained that I was determined to figure this out and let this sadness go. She understood, said she'd send me prayers and love.

Not more than 30 minutes later, the hotel phone rang and again expecting it to be Lisa, I said hello. It wasn't Lisa. It was another woman, an artist who knew a friend of mine who was an artist and a psychic in NYC. He'd just now called my office to get my hotel number. He must've called her immediately.

Obviously, she then immediately called me. Her opening words were, "You can't stay in Paris. I will come and get you and take you north out of the city to my country home."

My mind was swirling with strange emotions: doubt, psychic weirdness, synchronicities, and NO. I told her that I appreciated her offer but I wanted to see Paris. I wanted to be in Paris alone with my own thoughts and feelings. I could tell she was surprised and a little flummoxed that I didn't jump at her offer.

"My country home is a beautiful place. You'd like it there."
She hesitated and then said, "I don't think you should be in Paris."

"Why?"

"I don't know why exactly. I have a very strong feeling that I should take you away from the city."

"No, I'm staying."

This was another strong message from another woman that I had never met. What did this mean?

For the next week I walked the city. I cried and I sobbed. I sat at sidewalk cafes crying. No one approached to say a word to me.

One night, I tried to get back into the dream and tune into the woman I'd come to know through it. I feel like she was deeply in love and had turned her back on what was most meaningful to her. She must've earned the ire of the King since he took her home away. I am pretty sure I was decapitated shortly thereafter. I have always been fond of scarves to protect and cover my neck.

I walked and walked. I soaked up the art and beauty of Paris. Art museums, especially those that offered Rodin's sculptures, were heart-changing and glorifying all that was good and honest and loving. Paris was finally feeding my soul. I crossed and re-crossed bridges and walked along the Seine. Eventually I realized it must been a body memory that I couldn't shake until I went back to the "scene of the crime," so to speak. I reacquainted myself with a city I had once loved but had not loved me. Slowly, a little bit, day by day, I felt I could breathe deeply. The anxiousness lessened and I stopped crying.

I have never dreamed that dream again.

Since then, I have traveled to Paris and haven't cried once. Whatever the message and the hurt from the dream was healed and dealt with in my subconscious and my soul.

Christine came to visit me the next summer and cooked what became one of my favorites. Apricots and chicken breasts, pounded thin.

Chicken with Apricots

4 boneless chicken breasts split
1/2 cup dried apricots
White wine to cover
4 tablespoons butter, divided
1 clove garlic
1 tablespoon curry powder
1 teaspoon salt
Dash cayenne
1 cup chicken broth or stock
1/4 cup fresh lemon juice

1. Pound chicken breasts until they are about 1/4 inch thin.
2. Soak the apricots in water or white wine until soft
3. In a large fry or sauté pan, melt 1/2 the butter over medium heat: add the garlic, curry powder, salt and cayenne
4. Cook the herbs for 2–3 minutes, softening the garlic. Raise the heat and add the chicken and cook through, approximately 2–4 minutes per side.
5. After the chicken is cooked, remove to a plate.
6. Make the sauce: Add the chicken stock to the sauté pan and add lemon juice, the rest of the butter, and apricots. Reduce the heat to medium and let simmer until the apricots are softened.
7. Put the chicken back into the sauté pan and cover with the sauce.

Serves 4.

Healing Knees

Roasted Salmon
with Honey Glaze

John Cleese and Eric Idle were performing at Durham's Performing Arts Center (DPAC) in North Carolina. Seeing his name here and there and listening to interviews brought to mind my own stories about John.

John lives in London, but when I knew him, he lived in Santa Barbara, California. John was a big supporter of the Institute of Noetic Sciences (IONS) in Petaluma, California. In fact, it was Dean Radin, scientist/researcher at IONS and Marilyn Schlitz, president of IONS, who made the introduction. John was interested in hosting a series that investigated consciousness and the science of psi from his 'everyman' point-of-view.

It was seven or eight years ago that we started this dance. I'd call him and he'd be traveling; he'd call me and I'd be traveling or out in the garden. At that time, John was married to a Texas woman who had the most exaggerated Texan accent I've ever heard. We kept missing each other's phone calls. I talked with her so often I felt I knew her, although I never actually met her in person. Now they are divorced.

I attempted to reach him at the Carlyle Hotel in New York where he was staying when the Monty Python Broadway show,

Spamalot, opened. I called him and, sure enough, he wasn't in. His lovely Texan wife said he'd call me right back. He didn't—again—and so I forgot all about it. A few mornings later, a Sunday it was, I was showering and heard the phone ring and pondered; I'm almost done, not soapy, should I step out and answer the phone or should I just let the machine take it? I stepped out.

I tip-toed, dripping water across the bedroom floor, with only a towel around my head, and picked up the phone.

It was John Cleese apologizing profoundly for being so hard to catch-sounding exactly like John Cleese. We talked a bit about people we knew in common and then about the project.

His idea and point-of-view on the proposed documentary series, *Everyman's Guide to Enlightenment* was exactly parallel to my own: that is, that people feel a soul emptiness but don't realize where it is coming from and so fill their houses, heads, hearts and stomachs with stuff; the latest trends, commercial products and oh-by-the-way I'm sure that a successful business project will be the answer. They want happiness, an inner peace and a sense of fulfillment but are looking for it in all the wrong places.

Meanwhile, I was standing by my bed trying to air dry, feeling slightly strange even though he could never know (hopefully) that I was naked as a jay bird. I was listening carefully. After a bit, I was using the towel from my head to dry my body. A strange scene admittedly, but I was engaged totally in the conversation.

We talked about how, in our consumer society, materialism is not all it is built up to be and that it has not brought anyone lasting spiritual fulfillment.

That said, throughout the conversation—while saying that he wanted to do this project and that he thought it was important—he kept using one phrase; he had to make sure *his nut was covered*. You have to *understand about my nut,* he kept saying. And each time, I'd say okay, I understand. After 20 or 30 minutes I'd air-dried and laid down on my bed, stark naked and he is still talking about *covering his nut* and I'm thinking, "This is a Monty Python scene written by John Cleese right here."

We agreed to meet in New York City. We'd been passing, via email, all sorts of proposals and screen treatments, approved and blessed by him, and written by Marilyn Schlitz and Dean Radin. I had been busy having conversations with executives at HBO.

During the entire conversation I had a silly grin on my face and was grateful that I lived alone.

After a few discussions via conference calls and masses of emails, I received a message, HBO's interested in "your John Cleese project." I hustled to NYC to meet with him to talk about particulars and his "nut," by which he meant money.

My partner in this was Diane, late of A&E and The History Channel and Queen of Manhattan restaurants. John had wanted to go to Barney's, the department store with a great restaurant where others of his status and fame met for lunch. Diane wanted to go to the newest, hottest place on the Upper Eastside. A place whose name I've since forgotten.

It was one of those places with silk on the walls and heavy *silver* silverware and real china and crystal stemware. It was a tiny place with tables so close you could barely squeeze through. And prices not to be believed. You also had to have reservations weeks in advance. Diane's sister was a professional high-end restaurant diner so she got us a reservation. I thought, out loud, that maybe he'd be more comfortable in a place he was used to but Diane thought he'd be more impressed at the "newest hot restaurant."

Diane and I arrived early and were immediately seated. It was so damned tight between the tables that we could barely get our chairs out to sit and once sitting, there was no moving. Thank God, we were early. They would've had to move out several tables for the four of us to get seated at the same time.

John and his assistant arrived exactly on time and squeezed in. John is very tall, perhaps 6'4" or 6'5", so people all around him had to move a bit so he could pull his chair out. Meanwhile, the waiter hovered around trying to do everything he could to be helpful. The place was abuzz with "Isn't that John Cleese?"

We were finally settled and the table was gorgeous. It had every utensil imaginable and blocks of Himalayan pink salt; coasters for our glasses, for the flowers; pink salt was everywhere. John picked up everything on the table asking, "Whatever is this for? And this block of pink, whatever is this?" Salt, he was told. We were brought appetizers on blocks of pink salt. Salt and pepper for each of us on blocks of pink salt.

John joked with the waiter about the pink salt and asked, astutely, if the owner of the restaurant owned the pink salt company.

The waiter looked around and said hesitantly, "Yes, he does own the Himalayan Pink Salt Company."

Every comment, every observation was hilariously funny and even though I was certain John was wishing he wasn't there, he was such a good sport. I was grateful that he was also brilliant. We laughed our way though the meal.

His assistant was gracious. I expect he had seen everything imaginable. We talked business about HBO for a bit, but mostly we laughed.

John was clearly in his element and Diane and I were totally charmed and in love.

After our plates were cleared, he turned, looking directly at me and said very seriously, "I think you are a healer. I am certain you have healing power in your hands."

Over lunch we'd talked about our sun signs, somehow, although we discussed a range of subjects, he always returned the fact that we were Scorpios; he thought that was marvelous. Now and then he came back to my "healing ability." I said, "Everyone has some healing ability" and, "I'm sure I have a bit too, but who knows."

We'd had dessert and coffee. Every patron in the tiny restaurant had been listening to our entire conversation–there was not a sound anywhere except at our table. Finally, many of the tables were clearing out.

John turned to me with such a sincere and hopeful look in his eyes and said, "Would you put your hands on my knee to help my healing?"

I looked blankly at him.

He said, "I just had an operation on this knee and I need some healing energy."

Gosh, what could I say? He whipped his leg out from under the table, pulled his pant leg up and said, "Please, I know you're a healer."

I quietly said a prayer, rubbed my hands together and put them on John Cleese's right knee.

John Cleese was and is an impressive and brilliant man. I am grateful to have had that lunch with him, hands-on-knee healing and all.

In the end, HBO decided not to fund this project and we all moved on. He moved on, too. He divorced his Texan wife and moved back to London. I decided to stop working on my Life's Work and instead I began to take care of my Mom. Diane decided she'd like to learn about dating.

This is my take on the delicious salmon I had while sending healing energy to John Cleese's knee.

We both ordered this great salmon, which I adapted a bit.

Roasted Salmon with Honey and Mustard

1 large piece of skin-on salmon, approximately 1 lb.

½ cup whole grain mustard

2 tablespoons honey

2 tablespoons olive oil

Salt and pepper to taste

1 lemon, halved

4–5 Fresh thyme sprigs or 1 teaspoon dried thyme

1. Preheat oven to 450 degrees.
2. Whisk together the mustard, honey, olive oil, and salt and pepper to taste.
3. In a lightly oiled baking dish, place the salmon skin side down and pour the mustard mixture over salmon.
4. Cut the lemon in half. Slice a half into very thin slices and place over top of the salmon. (Save the remaining half to squeeze over salmon). Place fresh thyme springs on salmon or sprinkle the over top.
5. Bake in a hot, 450 degree oven, for 10 to 12 minutes or until cooked through. Remove from oven; squeeze the remainder of the lemon over the salmon.

Serve.

Lisa Moving to Manhattan
Crab and Artichoke Dip

My daughter, Lisa was living in Richmond, Virginia. She was excited about my move to Manhattan, especially after I called her, waking her up after midnight, to tell her that I'd spent the evening talking with the actor, *Richard Gere*. I was so energized and high with excitement I had to call her and spread it around. Once she was awake, she got as excited as me. I'd been at an event for the Dalai Lama and I happened to be seated next to Richard Gere. He was knowledgeable about Buddhism and had been a long time meditator. He was a great conversationalist and sincerely on the spiritual path. A sweet experience.

After I'd moved my office from my apartment on West 92nd Street to an official office at 52nd and Broadway, Lisa came to visit. She made a dip for a party I was having for a client and it was so good that everyone wanted to know the recipe, including me.

Lisa had recently gotten a divorce, after twelve years of marriage, from the love of her life. They met while in high school and they were as different as night and day but had a magnetic attraction to each other that just wouldn't quit no matter how many times they broke up. That difference—like night and day—finally overcame the magnetic attraction but it took twelve years.

Lisa would come to visit me in New York every now and then. I encouraged her to move to New York and work with me, but she said the city was too intense, too much for her sensitive Pisces soul. Finally, I asked her to come and stay for a few weeks, instead of just over a weekend. The "reason" was to help me with my taxes but, by then, she was more open to making the big move.

Lisa has a strong personality. At that time, she was also a real party girl. She had luxurious, long, thick, brown hair, expressive eyes with impossibly long eyelashes (we all wanted them) and an open and engaging personality. She loved to dance and have fun. Needless to say, she had a lot of fun dating in the Big Apple. Her social life became a source of endless entertainment for us in the office.

Lisa also had a wealth of business sense and office management skills that I didn't have and, most importantly, she was a delegator. Because I'd been doing everything, all the time, by myself, I wasn't good at allowing certain tasks to trickle down to my co-workers.

After working for me for a year and observing how things were going, she brought Karla to my office door. Karla initially came onboard as an intern for the documentary series on intuition we were producing, then we hired her to work full time on various projects we were developing. They stood there, in the doorway, looking at me.

"What?"

"Mom" she said, "You're paying Karla to do whatever you need her to do. Karla has a degree in filmmaking and can do anything you ask her to do. That is why you hired her."

She turned to Karla, "Karla, wouldn't you help her do anything she asked of you?"

Karla, of course said, "Yes."

"Mom, you do not have to do every single thing that needs to be done in this office. We are all here to work for you. You hired us. You pay us. You need to learn to delegate."

With a red face, I said, "You're right."

I got better at delegating. Although I know I had serious relapses.

Lisa was a godsend. One of the first things I asked her to do was take a lot of cash out to an Indian Reservation in Arizona. We were shooting the series on Intuition and the Native Americans wouldn't take checks. Lisa went to the bank, loaded up on hundred dollar bills and got on a plane and flew to Arizona.

She was forward-thinking, efficient and helped me every step of the way in whatever my endeavor was at the moment. She truly "had my back." That's a rare thing in life. After a few years of testing the waters, she started to take on literary clients and, thankfully, decided to start working as a Literary Agent. She was a natural and her clients loved her immediately.

Lisa was way more gracious than I. I could be a bit short and demanding. I didn't suffer fools gladly, as they say. I wasn't aware of my "challenging" personality at the time. Lately, I met someone who'd traveled to New York in the early 90s to pitch me her book project. She told me she had to sit on her trembling hands because she was so scared. "I'd heard about how hard you were..." Gosh, I had no idea.

Lisa now has her own literary agency, Lisa Hagan Literary and also a publishing company.

I am very proud of her.

This is the recipe that we've been making ever since she brought it with her to New York.

Crab and Artichoke Dip

2 cans (13 oz) artichoke hearts, cut into quarters

2 cups mayonnaise

1 cup grated parmesan cheese

½ cup chopped onion

1 pound of crabmeat

Salt and pepper to taste

1. Preheat the oven to 350 degrees.
2. Put the artichokes, mayonnaise, cheese and onion in a food processor and process until it is smooth with only a few small chunks remaining.
3. Pour into a bowl and gently add in the crab so as to not break up the lumps.
4. Pour into an attractive oven to table dish.
5. Bake at 350 for 20 to 25 minutes until golden and bubbly.

Serve with crackers or toast points.

Fear, Intense Fear

Hummus

From birth, I had an inordinate fear of snakes, a phobia really. When Mom was pregnant with me, she, Dad and Dad's younger brother, Berkley, were walking back from the tobacco field when Berkley spotted a snake down the lane. Berkley was terrified of snakes, so he and Mom stayed put. Dad walked down to whack it with a hoe. He killed it in short order.

It was a poisonous moccasin snake. Mom and Berkley hustled on down to make sure it was dead and pronounced it so. After Dad killed the snake, he used the hoe to pitch it into the field. It must've just had enough energy left to wrap itself around the handle of the hoe. When Dad pitched it, it went backwards and landed on Mom. The snake wrapped itself tightly around Mom's neck. Mom let out a blood-curdling scream. Dad rushed to get it off of her. Everyone thought that was why I was so afraid of snakes.

It made sense. We now know that emotions from the mother actually affect the child in the womb and she was a month or so away from giving birth to me. Somehow, I thought that there may be more to it than that but I had no idea what it could be.

As a child growing up on a farm with many creeks, springs, ponds and a river, there was an abundance of snakes. It seemed to me they were everywhere. And I kept an eye out for them. I was on hyper-alert for snakes most of my life.

In the course of things, I married, had children, and moved to the suburbs but I always continued my vigilance for snakes. Wherever I was or whenever I got in the car, I scanned to make sure it was free of snakes. It was a totally unconscious pattern.

My husband was the one and only person I ever knew who completely understood and never questioned my fear. When I had a nightmare, he would turn on the lights, look under the bed or clear out the closet. He'd do whatever it took to reassure me that the house was free of snakes. And that I was safe. He didn't try to placate me with, "they're more afraid of you then you are of them" and/or "they won't hurt you" -as if anyone could know that, for sure, for certain.

Dreams like that didn't happen often but it was one thing I could count on from him—a total understanding of that intense fear of snakes that I had endured all my life. Nevertheless, eleven years on, we got a divorce.

I met George Ritchie through a church group and we became fast friends. He wrote two books about his near-death experience, *My life After Dying: Becoming Alive to Universal Love* and *Ordered to Return; My Life After Dying.* Elizabeth Sherill co-wrote his first book, *Return from Tomorrow.* This following short paragraph I took from the back of *Return from Tomorrow* tells, in brief, Dr. Ritchie's story. "At the age of twenty, George Ritchie died in any Army hospital. Nine minutes later, he returned to life. What happened to him during those minutes was so compelling that it changed his life forever. He tells of his transforming encounter with the Son of God, who led him to encounters with other nonphysical beings at the very doorway of eternity. Ritchie's extraordinary experiences not only altered his view of eternity, but it has also altered the lives of hundreds of thousands of seekers. One of the most startling and hopeful descriptions of the realms beyond, this classic will inspire readers from all walks of life."

Through meeting Dr. Ritchie and listening to his story of dying and meeting Jesus, I learned about myself. My life developed a clarity that it had not had before and a clear focus. Every day was filled with deep meaning. What I wanted was to be closer to Jesus, the Christ. I realized that everything else that had happened in my life was just bringing me to that understanding.

But I was still afraid of snakes.

Dr. Ritchie said people that were coming to his office had a sickness of the spirit, not of the body, and he wanted to be able to help them in a deeper way. He organized summer camps high up in the mountains of Virginia for families. It was an intense, emotional, healing experience—if you were up to it.

I took my kids. It was good for us. I think we attended three years in a row. It was heavy with psychological counseling, spiritual lessons, and nature walks.

Late one night I was leaving my cabin, which was basically a screened in porch with bunk beds, to go to the bathroom. I opened the cabin door. I surprised a big snake. It lunged up at me, mouth wide open and fangs out ready to bite me. I turned around so quickly that my feet didn't move. My body fell forward, full weight onto the ground and I let out a blood curdling scream. Everyone came running. I calmed down, eventually, and finally went back to bed. Not that I shut my eyes all night. But I was quiet. Thinking.

The next morning, Dr. Ritchie found me and said let's go for a walk. Oh, no, I thought-another man telling me that snakes were more afraid of me than I of them and that, although the snake scared me, I'd scared it, too. Snakes are God's little creatures, too. Yeah. Yeah. I'd heard all of these explanations and more.

We started down the path towards the creek. Along the way, yes: Dr. Ritchie was telling me that snakes were God's creatures and that you scared him/her too, but he also took my hand and held it tight. Very tight. So tight that I ceased listening to him and began concentrating on my hand. Then he took my other hand. Ummm, I wondered, what is going on?

We stood together and he turned and said, "Look at me."

I looked up at him while trying to relax my hands which were hurting. He was explaining to me about fear and anxiety and how we use symbols for these things. He said I had huge amounts of both fear and anxiety; so consequently, I manifested a huge snake/fear. I projected my fear onto snakes. Then, he said, "Sandra, look down at the ground." I did. I was surrounded by snakes. They were crawling everywhere. Big snakes, baby snakes, green ones, black ones, all kinds of snakes. If I could've levitated I would've. No wonder he was holding me so tight, he knew I wanted to run, run like the wind, away from these snakes, like I'd done all my life, in my dreams. And a few times in real life, too.

I trusted Dr. Ritchie so completely that I didn't cry or scream or anything. I simply looked down and, for the first time, I saw that these snakes were relatively safe looking, calm, not trying to bite me, not threatening me in any way. They were just going about their business, probably wondering why Dr. Ritchie called them all together.

And then the light switched on—you know, that awakening that changes the structure of everything you thought you knew. I had an epiphany that, yes it was my fear within me that I had projected outwards. My fear took the form of a snake probably because of Mom's experience when I was in the womb. It really had nothing at all to do with the actual animal. It is me, all me, internalizing a super anxiety that has made me hyper vigilant for my entire life.

And like that, I let go of my fear of snakes. Though I never spoke throughout our walk, nor said a word about the release of fear, George felt the release and he let my hands go. We had a laugh. I rubbed my hands. The snakes crawled off; I didn't run.

George could do these things.

Months later after a brief meeting with my ex-husband to discuss the children, I returned to a friend's house for dinner. She hadn't yet arrived so I settled on her sofa to rest and went into a deep meditative state. I wondered about the connection from past lives that my husband and I might have had and what that meant to us now.

In that semi-sleep, altered state, I had a vision: a scene unfolded in front of me, as if it were projected on a big television screen except that it rolled horizontally, not vertically. In one scene, I was on a big barge floating down a river, dressed in a ceremonial, brocaded gown, one of many women similarly dressed. I knew that we were Asian, maybe from Siam, and my husband was in the royal family. His mother was at his knee attending his every need. We, the wives and ladies of the court, were ignored. I was sad, bored and leaning against a pole. I had my hand in the water. I watched as a snake swam up to the barge. I said to the snake, please bite me and take me away from here. Then I saw myself die.

Additional scenes rolled by which explained to me why my ex-husband was so understanding about my fear of snakes. In each and every scene, he is there and I die by snake bite.

In the last scene, I was a small black baby in the wilds of Africa, scared, crying, and sitting in the dirt. A snake is coming towards me and I'm looking at it fearfully. I say, in my mind, if you bite me I'll be forever afraid of snakes. As it bit me, a man was running towards me picking me up. It was my husband in the body of an almost naked black man.

Amazingly enough, I continue to have snake dreams, but they are no longer fear-based. Now my dreams reflect a much larger understanding of the history, meaning and spirituality of the snake—but that is for another time.

I find hummus to be a soothing food and it is great for parties.

Hummus

I made hummus all kinds of ways with all kinds of beans and peas. I use whatever I happen to have.

For the beans, I have experimented with navy beans or black-eyed peas mixed with a foundation of chickpeas (if we had lots of people coming) and often didn't use tahini but a teaspoon or two of soy sauce.

Because I had so many herbs, I'd include ½ cup of parsley or basil, a little rosemary, oregano-whatever looked and smelled good to me on that day. The herbs made it lighter and fresher.

When using the herbs I put them in right at the end so they aren't shredded and you can see what they are. Sometimes I chopped the herbs up and mixed them in after the food processor had done its job.

2 cups drained well-cooked or canned chickpeas, liquid
    reserved
$\frac{1}{2}$ cup tahini (sesame paste), optional,
    with some of its oil
$\frac{1}{4}$ cup extra-virgin olive oil, plus oil for drizzling
2 cloves garlic, or to taste
Salt and freshly ground black pepper to taste
1 tablespoon ground cumin or paprika, or to taste, plus a
    sprinkling for garnish
Juice of 1 lemon, plus more as needed
Chopped fresh parsley leaves for garnish

1. Put everything except the parsley in a food processor and begin to process; add the chickpea liquid or water as needed to allow the machine to produce a smooth puree.
2. Taste and adjust the seasoning (I often find I like to add much more lemon juice). Serve, drizzled with the olive oil and sprinkled with a bit more cumin or paprika and some parsley.

Discovery Dreams
Spinach Lasagna

My friend Teresa makes the best spinach lasagna. It is a dependable and delicious meal and doesn't take much time to assemble when you have all the ingredients on hand.

She was a feature writer, art and celebrity profiles mostly, for the Norfolk, Virginia newspaper. She is tiny, blond, extremely curious and a complete non-conformist. We'd often have lunch together when I worked at WHRO, the local PBS station in the Norfolk, Virginia Beach area. This was during the time I was having a long series of dreams about Ted Turner. Yes, <u>that</u> Ted Turner. Always the reporter she wanted to know every detail of the dreams, questioning me repeatedly about what I thought they could mean. Later, she told me that she made notes of my dreams. She had a feeling that maybe someday those dream would come true. I never could make heads or tails of them at the time.

Following is a feature story she wrote about me after she attended the premier of my Discovery Channel series, *The Power of Dreams*. The party was in New York City. Now retired, at that time Teresa was a staff writer for The Sunday Break in *The Virginian Pilot* and *Ledger Star*.

The Sunday Break, *The Virginian-Pilot* & *Ledger-Star,* June 19, 1994

The Power of Dreams
by Teresa Annas, Staff Writer

Seven years ago, Sandra Martin was having lunch at Kelly's on Colley Avenue in Norfolk, telling a friend about her dream.

"I dreamed I was dancing with Ted Turner," Martin said. She thought the dream was telling her something. But she didn't think it predicted she'd waltz with the Turner Broadcasting mogul.

To Martin, the dream indicated she should enter the field of television production.

"I know it's crazy," said Martin. She was 39, had no college education and was selling underwriting for WHRO, the region's public broadcasters. Granted, she was an award-winning sales-person. And she was well read. But she had zero contacts in the realm of network or cable producers.

Still, she felt compelled to make the effort.

Today at 8 p.m., her three hour series, "The Power of Dreams," premieres on The Discovery Channel. Martin is executive producer for the series, a multimillion-dollar production that takes viewers around the world—Greece, India and Australia—to look at the purpose and potential of dreams. Musician Billy Joel, author William Styron and His Holiness the XIV Dalai Lama are among those featured.

"The average person devotes 50,000 hours in a lifetime to dreaming," said Clark Bunting, Discovery's senior vice president of programming, explaining what sold Discovery—which has 61 million subscribers—on the series. "Everybody dreams. And there are some fascinating stories. Did you know that George Patton dreamed of fully developed battle plans? And Abe Lincoln dreamed of his assassination?"

In the series, the Dalai Lama tells about dreams he's had

about his 17th century predecessor, the fifth Dalai Lama. Billy Joel reveals that "all of the music I've composed has come from a dream. I dream sounds, arrangements, solos." Styron discusses how the heroine of *Sophie's Choice* came to him in a dream.

The show examines how other cultures—from Australia's aboriginal people to Tibetan Buddhist monks—use dreams in their lives. The dream world proclaims as an on-camera monk says, "it is the place where you can discover yourself."

Following her dreams

Certainly, self-discovery was part of the process for Martin as she began concocting her dream series in the late 1980s, while still living part time in Virginia Beach.

She was a few years into her Ted Turner dream phase. "I had those dreams on and on for the longest time. They really kept me going," said Martin, who moved full time to Manhattan in 1990.

Earlier this month, Martin sat bathed in late afternoon sun in her midtown Manhattan office, located near the producers, network executives and book publishers with whom she does business. Surrounded by new age art, Oriental rugs and books on dreams and women's issues, she discussed her unusual, dream-directed career path.

Dream after dream, "I'd be signing contacts with Ted Turner. I'd be doing deals with Ted Turner. Dancing with Ted Turner. At one point I got married to Ted Turner."

The message was so strong; she actually called Turner's Atlanta office. Amazingly, she ended up on the phone with Turner himself.

"So I talked to him about these programs I wanted to do on paranormal science. He was the nicest guy. He said, "Sounds real interesting to me. Come on down and we'll talk about it."

Martin flew to Georgia, only to find Turner had flown off with Raquel Welch. But she learned enough to realize Turner

Broadcasting was not likely to spend big bucks to produce the series she had in mind.

"But I went down there to see him, based on these dreams. I just wanted to believe that Ted Turner would swoosh into my life and let me make all these programs I wanted to do."

In another dream, she and Turner were eating fried chicken in his office as the two signed contracts. Books and television scripts were piled high on his desk.

Martin had that dream before she found her niche as a literary agent, too. Since 1988, she has sold several dozen books to major publishers. She recently sold a book by Virginia Beach psychotherapist Scott Sparrow for a six-figure sum.

Finally, a dream came that put it all in perspective.

"I was coming out of this house with Jason Robards. We walked across this big field together, arm in arm. At one point, I'm talking to him and look up and he's turned into Ted Turner.

"So we walked across this hill and there's a wide river—vast, blue and beautiful. And this really large American flag was in the river. Both of us were appalled by that. So we waded out in the river and pulled it out. We walked up that riverbank to where the flagman was."

In her dream, they got the flagman to raise the flag. As the two walked away, Turner asked her if she'd go to work for him.

Yes, she said. "But I told him I wouldn't be his secretary. I would only be his equal. He said, "OK."

With that dream, she realized Turner had represented her all along. At first, she was acting the role of agent and producer—symbolized by Robards, a great actor.

Finally, she gained real power.

But she saw more in the dream.

"I really felt the spirit of America had gone down the river, so to speak. And wanted, in some way, to bring the spirit back.

"We are such a great nation. But we've gotten so cynical. So afraid. So scared. Scared of standing up for what's right.

"I want the hero to come back. I want the good guys to be valued.

"So all the things I do, or want to do, are those kinds of things.

Farm Family

Martin's life experiences have shaped her direction.

She grew up on a farm in Bracey, Va., just below South Hill, where she and her three siblings worked hard in the fields and cared about their neighbors. Once a month, a minister would sermonize for her kin in the tiny chapel on their property.

The family was filled with avid readers with willful personalities.

The independent-minded Martin married at age 16 and bore a son and a daughter. Her marriage broke up after 11 years; by then, she was a wealthy young wife and mother living in Richmond.

Vast change would ensue.

One major event was surviving an aircraft crash in the Grand Canyon in August of 1974. Amazingly, the single-engine airplane glided without engine for a soft crash landing atop a mesa by the canyon's rim.

"That changed the way I felt about the people around me. How I embraced them after that. You realize what's important to you. And what was important to me was living.

"Really living. I couldn't live my life through anyone else. And I didn't want to die with any regrets."

She moved to Virginia Beach in November of that year and began her odyssey. Within a few months she was lecturing on dreams for the Association of Research and Enlightenment.

By the mid-1980s, she was experimenting with television. She produced her own low-low-budget talk show, "The Sandra Martin Show," which aired on Cox Cable's public affairs channel. One segment was on dreams.

Then she had this dream about riding a helicopter to the roof of a big house, which she entered from the top through a narrow opening.

True to her dream, Martin entered a tight field—starting at the top.

"Monumental effort"

Recently, several hundred producers, writers, television executives and media representatives gathered at The Asia Society in New York for a screening of "The Power of Dreams."

Sipping wine and sodas, producers who worked with Martin described her as an unusually easy going executive producer—approachable, charming.

"She's such a mild-mannered Virginia gal, who attracts this wide range of people," said Katherine Carpenter, series producer and frequent PBS producer. She recalled a party invitation from Martin that claimed guest would include astral projectors, cowgirls, levitators and alien abductees.

"Sandra's great—ebullient, bubbly—and has tons of ideas," Carpenter said. "And this is a ground-breaking series. And I would call it an enormous achievement that she was able to get the series off the ground. It's been a monumental effort."

Martin was "really the sine qua non," or essential ingredient, behind the series, said Linda Harrar, who produced that introductory hour.

The odds are against a first time producer landing a three-hour series, she said. "But good ideas can break down a lot of walls. Particularly when they're presented well—and forcefully."

"She is so unusual," added Veronica Young, a third producer. "She came out of left field and just plunged in. She has terrific innocence. She's not jaded. It's a healthy naiveté. She doesn't expect problems, and she seems determined to prevail."

"And she has huge charm."

"Sometimes," said Young speaking in a confidential tone, "She gets people to open their checkbooks."

It was Martin's night. She floated from group to group, introducing her parents—who still farm in Bracey—to her dream team.

Later, before the lights went down to preview selected portions of the series, Discovery's Denise Baddour, a senior vice president, shared her thoughts with the crowd.

"I would like to acknowledge the woman who brought this series to us," she said. "Sandra Martin, would you please stand up?"

The applause was loud and long—almost surreal. After all, the moment capped a dream she had held onto for so long.

All she could do was stand up and smile.

"She just wouldn't give up," said Baddour. "And I'm glad she didn't."

Teresa's Lasagna is easy to make and delicious. I have shared her recipe with many friends.

Teresa's Spinach Lasagna

Prep time: 15 minutes Cook time: One hour

Take six lasagna noodles; don't cook them, just rinse them in cool water and set aside.

15 oz container ricotta cheese

10 oz box frozen chopped spinach, thawed and
     well-drained

8 oz of mozzarella

26 oz of spaghetti sauce—whatever kind you prefer,
     whether plain or fancy, cheesy or not

1. Preheat the oven to 350 degrees.
2. Spread enough sauce on bottom of a rectangular baking dish to cover
3. Spread 3 washed noodles, side by side over the sauce—they fit perfectly.
4. Mix the ricotta and spinach together.
5. Spread ½ of the spinach and ricotta mixture on the noodles.
6. Spread ½ of the mozzarella on the spinach ricotta
7. Pour ½ of the container of spaghetti sauce over the cheeses.
8. Now, repeat the layering process of noodles, cheese and sauce.
9. Cover with foil and cook for 45 minutes at 350 degrees.
10. Take foil off and cook 15 more minutes until brown, bubbly and crispy on top.

Serves 6.

Coincidence, I think Not!
Shrimp Fra Diavolo

One of my heroes is Bill Moyers of PBS and author of numerous books and essays, not only on current affairs, but on spirituality and the human quest. I have followed his PBS interview series for years. The reason Bill was my hero was because of documentaries he'd made: *Joseph Campbell and the Power of Myth*; *A Gathering of Men with Robert Bly* and now *Healing and the Mind*.

Another one of my heroes was John Fetzer of the Fetzer Foundation, now called the Fetzer Institute located in Kalamazoo, Michigan. John was the owner of the Detroit Tigers. He sold the team in 1981. He owned radio and television stations. He developed a directional antenna for broadcasting at night that changed radio. He started Fetzer Cablevision, which became Charter Communications. He was a media mogul.

In private, John Fetzer was a closet mystic. He meditated, investigated metaphysical subjects, contemplated deep philosophy and explored all types of non-western healing. He was curious, funny, and full of life. Both Bill Moyers and John Fetzer were invested in the future of humanity from a deeply spiritual and consciously unifying perspective.

Bill had sent a proposal to The Fetzer Foundation to fund a new series he'd developed on alternative health. I was friends with people at Fetzer and had spent some time in Mr. Fetzer's office talking about the most perceptive psychics and research about psi abilities, near death and dreams. This discussion was in his newly-built sustainable and perfectly aligned and designed building in Kalamazoo, Michigan.

I'd been involved with the Fetzer Foundation since the late 80s. Now it was the early 90s and, a few months before I had been in Kalamazoo talking about a book project on Mr. Fetzer's life. After our business discussion, he said he had one more question. He handed me a proposal from Bill Moyers: what did I think about this proposal and did I think it would be good for them and good for the public? I scanned it, read a bit of it and enthusiastically endorsed Mr. Moyer's proposal and the project. In my mind, anything Bill Moyers did would be good.

A new Manhattan friend, a producer for a well-known prestigious PBS series, had talked me into calling Bill Moyers about my own series I'd been working on. It was my dream project; a series about dreams. I'd spent years interviewing researchers, attending conferences on dreams, reading everything I could find on dreams in order to create an eight-hour television documentary series. The series addressed compelling dream concepts: what do dreams mean, how they shape our lives, why we can't remember them, and how they expose our past and show us the future. And I'd had no takers. So far.

My new friend, this PBS producer was straight out of central casting for a hard-nosed, outspoken, in your face and don't-mess-with-me kind of woman. With hands on hips she said, "Sandra you have to be bold, step forward, tell your story. This isn't the South; no one is going to ferret you out to discover your specialness. You know Bill Moyers is interested in the same fields you are, so just pick up the phone and call him." She was scary but always gave me solid advice.

I called Bill; the Mr. Bill Moyers. It was hard but I did it. He called me back on March 16th, 1990 and we had a wide-ranging conversation about the future of alternative health, ESP and PBS funding. He said he'd sent a proposal to Fetzer Foundation and was anxious to hear from them. Although I didn't tell him that the board had already approved funding his series, I was very encouraging.

I did tell him about my proposed dream series and he sounded interested but he didn't quite "get" it. I was nervous and I expect I explained it poorly. Nevertheless, it was a productive conversation. I was beside myself with excitement—I talked with Bill Moyers!

The next day a friend, Teresa (the one that was a writer for the Norfolk papers), came to visit and we walked up to an Italian restaurant near 8th Avenue on 57th Street for lunch. We were just seated and when I looked up from my menu, there I was sitting directly across from Bill Moyers. I was in awe and could barely pay attention to my Shrimp Diavolo and, even though Teresa encouraged me to walk over and introduce myself, I just couldn't.

She said "You just talked to him on the phone yesterday!"

I kept saying, "Who am I to interrupt his lunch?"

And so I didn't. If it had happened a few years later I would've gone right over and said hi, but then I was shy and felt unworthy.

His documentary series aired in 1993, *Healing and the Mind* funded by Fetzer. This is what he said in an interview: "There's definitely a zeitgeist building," says Moyers of the growing interest in alternative medicine, "and I wanted to explore it—skeptical but open-minded."

This is my take on the Shrimp Diavolo I had while keeping an eye on Bill Moyers.

Shrimp Diavolo

1 pound large shrimp, peeled and deveined

1 teaspoon salt

1 teaspoon crushed red pepper flakes

2–3 tablespoons olive oil

2 tablespoons butter

1 small onion, chopped

2 cloves garlic, minced

Chopped fresh parsley

1. Put on water to boil to cook pasta—spaghetti or linguini—whatever type you prefer is good.
2. Toss 1 pound large shrimp, peeled and deveined with 1 tsp salt and 1 tsp of crushed red pepper flakes.
3. Put 2 or 3 tablespoons of olive oil and 2 tablespoons of butter in a skillet and cook shrimp lightly turning to cook evenly. Take the shrimp out of the pan.
4. Sauté 1 small chopped onion and 2 minced cloves of garlic for about 5 minutes until translucent.
5. Simmer until the sauce thickens; put the shrimp back into the sauce and stir in the fresh parsley.
6. Serve with pasta.

Serves 4.

Intuition Synchronicity

Ginger Ale

Don't you wish, like I wished, there was a way to know for sure whether those hunches, that feeling in your gut, those little intuitive nudges from within, were real or not? Don't you wish you knew when to rely on a hunch, hoping it isn't wish fulfillment? How do we know the difference between these all too human feelings and true psychic and intuitive impulses?

I was always torn. I have had so many intuitive moments and most often I did not follow through on them. The result was always to my detriment. You're reading about the few that I did follow. And I am extremely grateful for those few.

Because of my own experiences, I decided to make a serious investigation on the subject of Intuition. I researched and interviewed all the finest researchers, from psychologists to biological scientists to parapsychologists. And I interviewed all the top intuitives and psychics.

My intuition television series is the result of years and years of work looking for the intuition answer. Is it real? Can you count on it?

This is one intuitive moment I had.

A good friend insisted I join New York Women in Film (NYWIF), an organization for women who made television and filmmaking their careers. It'd be good for my career, she'd advised. Besides, I'd insisted she join the FIONS-Friends of the Institute of Noetic Sciences board. I did and I learned a lot, met film and television executives, and enjoyed the monthly programs. I'd produced a few documentaries for PBS, Discovery & TLC but I made the majority of my income from being a literary agent.

Documentaries are hard to get funding for—at least the ones I wanted to make. They take rigorous dedication to be brought to completion. When I'd wanted to make a series on dreams, every gatekeeper or developer for every network/cable outlet—and they were all men at the time—said the same thing: "What are you going to do, put a camera in somebody's head?"

"Well, no, I'm not. Dreams are all about symbols."

And then there was the most common rejection: "No one has ever produced a television series on dreams."

So there you go! No one has done one and that is the end of that! Finally, after many years of working on it, Discovery said yes to the project after they'd said no three times. I am persistent when I truly believe in something. *The Power of Dreams* aired on The Discovery Channel in 1995 and has aired on all their other channels since then. It was also sold as a DVD to colleges and universities.

Making a documentary is not an easy task. First, you identify an excellent idea that works for television. It must be an idea that can be visualized with telegenic and articulate characters that can also be easily edited. Most of television these days is story-telling in seven minute segments. You also want an idea that had been produced in the past but not lately, an update, or an idea that is trending at the moment, or idea that you know is being produced for a competitor network, and rarely, but occasionally a brand new idea that has never been done. Then you do your research, interview the experts, write a broad overview of the concept and characters, develop a treatment, and hopefully finish with an award-winning, surefire proposal. After that extended period, where you've put your heart and soul into something you believe in, you research the media field, searching for an appropriate media outlet in the vast Cable TV, Network TV and now internet television sites. If you can't find a media deal, then you will look for public funding or foundation funding so that you can attract producers and directors. With money in hand, at last, the real work begins.

In the late-90s, I decided that a documentary on intuition was the next television series I wanted to produce so I wrote a detailed proposal. After a couple of years of very hard work, and after the now vastly larger field of media outlets had all said no repeatedly, I'd managed to secure private funding.

It was to be a mini-series, three one-hour documentaries on everything you might ever want to know about Intuition and now I was looking for producers who shared a "like mind." This was before the "paranormal" trend hit television and intuition was the code word for psychic ability. I'd put together a wish list of what I wanted that producer to be: aware of the material, sensitive to the intuitives and the researchers, and maybe, hopefully, one that would make my Minnesota funder comfortable.

I had a gut feeling about the New York Women in Film–(NYWIF). I kept getting that inner voice, a nudge to go to a meeting soon. So I decided that at the next NYWIF meeting I'd pass the word that I was looking for a producer-as NYWIF was the mother lode of women freelance producers. The meeting was for the screening of a film by Sally Field.

When I got there, a producer for HBO I vaguely knew came over and said I have someone that I think you'd like to meet. We couldn't find her right then and while we were looking around, having our wine and cheese, I told her about the documentary series I was planning and about this amazing funder. He was an inventor and made millions using his "intuition." He was an eccentric and complicated fellow living on a huge estate in Minnesota.

I told her I'd hoped to find a producer/director who was familiar with intuition, writing/producing and talking with folks from Minnesota. I knew this was going to be hard to do, and I didn't have much hope for it, but I thought I'd give it a shot-you know using intention, putting it out there and believing.

She rolled her eyes, "Wow, that is a big order. Good luck with that Sandra." We walked to the auditorium to listen to Sally Field.

The screening was starting and I still hadn't met my friend's new acquaintance. As we were going to our seats, she happened to walk by and we were introduced. Mary Katzke was a tall, slender, pale, blond beauty with flawless skin. We talked briefly, hello, how are you, she moved on with her friends and my HBO friend and I settled in to listen to Sally.

After the film, I looked for Mary but didn't see her so I went out to get a taxi. It was pouring rain. Every taxi was taking more than one passenger. I got in line for the next one going across town. The doorman opened the door of the taxi and I pulled myself in trying to avoid getting soaked, looked across the seat and there was Mary Katzke.

We laughed, "This is a funny coincidence."

We sat dripping and made small talk. I asked her what she did and she said she was writing a play.

"What's it about?"

"Intuition. It's about how intuition can change your life. In fact, that's my title, Intuition."

"Ummm. How'd you get to New York City?"

"I moved here from Alaska but I grew up in Minnesota. And I'm really a documentary producer. I made a film on the oil spill of the Exxon Valdez, which won many awards for which I'm extremely grateful. But I've always wanted to write for the theatre so I moved to the Big Apple."

We were close to her destination she said, "By the way, I need work if you know of any."

As amazing as that was all by itself, getting in the taxi with her, it was nothing compared to our conversation. Mary was familiar with intuition, was originally from Minnesota, was available, and was an award winning documentary producer-the more astounding part was this: I'd been a judge for PBS documentaries that year and I'd been impressed by her documentary and voted for it. I'd suggested that they air it on PBS's award winning series, POV. I loved her professional and equal-handed documentary on the Exxon Valdez oil spill.

"Mary, here's my card, please fax me your resume."

The taxi stopped, she got out and said goodbye.

All the way to my apartment, my head was swimming. I kept saying, what synchronicity, what magic. I walked through my lobby, in a daze, wondering how this happens. I took the elevator 35 floors up and plopped down on my sofa. Just damn amazing. Life is good. Magic happens. But ever the pragmatic, I thought well, we'll just see how it all works out.

Mary Katzke turned out to be a dynamic producer/writer and knew how to talk with our Minnesotan funders. She was fascinated by intuition. Our series ran on PBS as a PBS Pledge Week Special and was aired in Europe. Afterwards, she moved back to Alaska. New York is a tough town.

We were all about healthy foods and green drinks at that time. I'd stop on the way to work many mornings and have a one-ounce green shot at the local health food store. All sorts of natural drinks that seemed like they should be easy to make but I found they were time consuming and a lot of work. Later, I decided that green drinks were way too much trouble and Ginger Ale kind of "spoke to me."

Homemade Ginger Ale

Wow, was that easy!

1 cup peeled, finely chopped fresh ginger
2 cups water
Sparkling water to taste
Honey to taste

1. Fresh lemon juice to taste
2. Bring the water to a boil. Add the ginger, drop the heat to medium, and simmer for 5 minutes
3. Take it off the heat and strain, saving the syrup and discarding the ginger.
4. Mix 1 part ginger syrup and 3 parts sparkling water with a little honey or a squeeze of lemon juice mix and pour over ice.

Serve.

Events at the Dairy Barn
Speakers and Recipes

The following chapters are based on a few of the speakers that we invited to speak at the Dairy Barn.

These unique events came to pass because, when my old New York friends visited my home, I'd invite my new Lake Gaston friends to come and meet my literary clients and old friends. Often these parties ended up being lectures, some with slide presentations. My new friends would ask me if I thought—whoever...a friend or client of mine whose book they'd recently read would come and give a talk. Of course they would.

I enjoyed this give and take because I love to entertain and I loved my clients. They were extraordinary writers, researchers and spiritual seekers. These new friends were hungry for new ideas, new ways of understanding life. Like most people, they wonder why we're here on planet earth, what it means and how it all works. I had clients who'd written books that answered many of those questions. Our gatherings were full of energy, excitement and questions.

But the first thing I wanted to do was start a garden. I started with three beds, each a few yards long and 40 inches across.

Wide enough for me to be able to reach across to plant seeds or put in starter plants from the greenhouse and then pull weeds and hopefully harvest yummy vegetables.

I had clean organic compost and dirt without chemicals brought in to fill the beds. The dirt called to me to put my hands in it, run it through my fingers, smell it and plant seeds. I had no idea that the small garden and the farming life would call to me so passionately. The year before I had been a city girl and loved Manhattan, loved the life I'd been living. But I gratefully adapted like I'd never been away for 40 years!

At first I planted a variety of veggies and all my new and old friends oohed and aahed at how delicious and bright they tasted.

As more and more clients came to visit, it became clear that my home wasn't large enough to accommodate everyone. We, my sister Brenda and I, decided to renovate the Dairy Barn which was right beside my garden. The family home place was and is still a working farm. There were huge open sided barns full of hay and four silos full of soy beans and wheat. The plowed fields began right behind the Dairy Barn and extended for many acres.

The hilly fields sloped down into a depression where a creek had been and it was where my sister Brenda had a pond made. It made for a pretty view and good fishing. Rolling green hills and blue sky shared with good friends. That sounded like a perfect combination.

We decided to re-claim the Dairy Barn in the name of Books and Speakers. Of course, we asked my Mom, Florence Martin, whose farm it was now that Dad had died if that was okay. She said, "I think it is a great idea."

The Instigators and Workers

Florence Martin

My Mom, Florence Ferrell Martin is an innovative, smart and strong-willed woman. Her determination could rival that of Genghis Kahn. When she made up her mind to do something or for you to do something, it was a done deal. She was also a gracious and charming southern woman.

Mom had always been a spiritual seeker and a devoted student of the Bible. Mom re-instituted the Martin family's Primitive Baptist Church in Bracey. When I was a child there weren't enough local members to warrant a minister coming from North Carolina to preach so instead we drove there once a month. We attended churches in Rocky Mount, Jacksonville and, the nearest one, Memorial Primitive Baptist Church at Stem.

Primitive Baptist followers were a different kind of folk. They believed in predestination and in salvation by grace, not works. The Elders only spoke to the congregation when they had been "called to preach." If they weren't "called" we sat for the hour and sang hymns. Many years later I saw people channeling and realized that was what our Elders had been doing. They believed that the dreams and visions described in Biblical times still happened today. They preached in a sing-song rhythm but it could never ever put you to sleep as it was a message preached loudly and with grim determination. It was a powerfully spiritual place.

Mom thought it was time to re-ignite our spiritual roots and power up our beautiful little Church. Everyone was glad that she did. Our Church, simply built, enclosing one large room was a white clapboard building with our family graveyard behind it. It was stark in its beauty, with no piano or organ, and no adornments. It was plain and simple. It was constructed by my Dad's father, and his father's brothers in 1923. The pine they used hadn't fully cured and as a child I'd looked up at my grandfather and great-grandfather's hand prints sealed in the pine resin, on the ceiling and on the benches. Even as a child I was awed by that. My great-grandfather was buried in the graveyard behind the Church. Many years later, I remember thinking how amazing it was that I never noticed that he and I were born on the same day, October 30th, almost a hundred years apart.

Mom first was introduced to the A.R.E. when she was Director of the Virginia State Travel Center on Interstate 85. Edgar Cayce was a world-famous psychic who died in 1945. He gave over 14,000 readings; over 9,000 on health and healing and others on Atlantis, Jesus, past lives, dreams, and many other topics. After that introduction, Mom took her vacation time to attend A.R.E. conferences. That was as long as Mr. Irion was one of the speakers. Everett Irion was her guide and teacher. Mr. Irion was the Director of Finance and now my sister Brenda has that job. Mom believes all is divinely ordered and this was meant to be.

My Mom has been an inspiration to so many in our community and is deeply loved and appreciated. After retiring from the Travel Center, she opened a bookstore and mineral and gem shop. For many years she held Bible study groups, Course in Miracles study groups, Search for God study groups and more at her little bookstore in South Hill, Virginia.

Brenda and I are following in her path.

Brenda Butler

Brenda had worked for many years at an international company as head of their accounting and finance department. When that company merged with another larger company, she had the opportunity to be bought out. She'd been there a long time. She took the money. The merger afforded her two years to concentrate on working on the Dairy Barn.

Brenda is the adventurer of our family. She yearns for new

experiences, plans sensibly for them and does all that is necessary to made sure she is capable and strong enough for the extreme climbs or work involved. She has taken vacations in China and South America since she'd already seem most of Europe. She also takes working vacations in state and national parks to clean and rebuild. She is a generous and loving soul. Brenda has traveled all over the world and continues to entertain us with her travel stories. We are in awe of her and what she does.

Without Brenda, the re-invention of the Dairy Barn would not have happened. With her determination, her hard work, inside and outside painting, moving boxes and bookcases, and creating a welcoming front entrance, she made it an exciting adventure for all of us.

After a couple of years, she decided to go back to work. She is now Finance Director of A.R.E. in Virginia Beach.

Lisa Hagan

Lisa was and is the go-to gal. She knows how to make things happen and jumps in and plows on through to the end. Sometimes I get tired just watching her. She took over the Literary Agency in 2001 and loves her life working with writers in spiritual, alternative health and UFO/ancient mysteries fields. After New York, she spent time living in London, and eventually she landed here in Bracey. She had lots of great ideas for the Dairy Barn.

JoAnn and Buck Courter

Two new Lake Gaston friends were integral to making the Dairy Barn the success it turned into: Buck and JoAnn Courter. JoAnn and I had met after my hairdresser gave me her name and number saying "I think you two would hit it off" and we did.

JoAnn and Buck were from upstate New York and moved to Lake Gaston via Colorado, Florida and Raleigh. They were both artists. Buck could do anything but his specialty was stained glass. His work should be hanging in museums. JoAnn is also an artist in mosaics and glass. I have a small blue dish she made my Mom right by the computer. They are also world-class cooks.

They loved the idea for the Dairy Barn project and they both have a superior can-do attitude. Buck did a lot of the heavy lifting and he also painted an inviting image of cows in pastures on the front of the building and gnomes in a forest scene for our bookstore. JoAnn is a hard worker and has a zillion great ideas for just about anything. She is an interior decorator at heart and at business. We worked well together.

Making it Happen

The Dairy Barn is a cement block, sturdy building that originally was for milking our herd of Holstein dairy cows but, after the dairy cows were sold, it was used for storage; wheat, fertilizer, whatever my farmer brother needed it for. He was fine with making it into a space for speakers and helped with whatever we needed. With huge amounts of elbow grease, hard labor and, of course, money, we converted it into a nice place to have speakers share their wisdom.

We painted those cement block walls multiple times. It seemed they just soaked up the paint and looked just like before. It was hard work but we persevered. And we laughed a lot. We brought over church pews from our church and put together bookcases for books. Most of the books and all of the Tom Clark collectibles were from Mom's closed bookstore.

I thought I'd sell fresh vegetables.

It was exciting and we were ready. Of course, we didn't have bathrooms and the roof was tin and oh, that's right, we had no heat or air conditioning. Other than that it was great.

At first, our speakers were my literary clients. I'd either sold their books through my literary agency, Paraview Literary or published their books at my first publishing imprint, Paraview Books or, after that, at my Simon and Schuster imprint, Paraview Pocket Books. Lisa asked her literary clients to come and speak. We invited local alternative health care providers: Reiki masters, massage therapists, counselors and therapists of all types, dream teachers, spiritual teachers and later, when I joined the Board of The Rhine Center based in Durham, North Carolina, parapsychology researchers.

Recipes

I created many of the recipes during that time of abundant vegetables for grateful and enthusiastic eaters! Other recipes were tried and true ones that I've been cooking for a long, long time.

Events

Our events were on Saturday mornings. Our speaker's presentation would begin at 10:30. Each speaker was different; an entertaining story from a local practitioner, a spiritual teaching from a writer or minister, alternative healing methods or life lessons learned. Each speaker shared with us their own experiences about their spiritual journey. We encouraged new speakers. Each was heartfelt and appreciated. We had created a safe space to share the most sacred stories.

The Dairy Barn Events began operation during the summer of 2005 and closed its doors in the fall of 2011 when we finally moved our events to Ellie Newbauer's home in Littleton, North Carolina. Ellie, a spry, sassy and profound spiritual teacher, had been one of our speakers and a late comer to our group. She'd helped to start Unity Church in Richmond. She shared with us her dream of creating a retreat center at her home on Lake Gaston.

Ellie was a gift from heaven for us. We loved the Dairy Barn but, while absolutely wonderful when the sky was in harmony, we had to admit it was not so good when it rained or stormed. A tin roof with no insulation meant no one could hear the speaker during summer rain storms. Also, since we had no heat, we only had events during warm months and everyone wanted to get together more often. I often had speakers come to my home during the colder months but it wasn't large enough for everyone. Ellie had a home that was created for weekend events.

While I was gardening and entertaining and putting together Events at the Dairy Barn (that's how I titled them), I was also working to start a new television network that focused on deep spirituality, consciousness and alternative health. Even though I gave up pretty much everything to make that happen, it did not. It broke my heart because I believed it was what I was meant to do next. Life goes on.

Dairy Barn Events continue on at Ellie's home where we have what we've come to call "First Sunday." Every first Sunday of the month, Ellie leads us in prayer and meditation. If we have one, we enjoy a speaker, and if not, we have a discussion based on an inspirational passage or a question that each of us answers in his or her own way. Afterwards we have a big potluck lunch and endless fascinating conversations. Some of our past events are listed on our Facebook page under Bracey Dairy Barn.

Unfortunately, my computer has crashed a few times and I've lost many of the Dairy Barn records. Most of this information to follow came from my Mom. In a casual conversation I told her that I didn't have many of the documents from the Dairy Barn, except for photographs I'd taken.

Mom went searching and shortly supplied me with many of the flyers that I'd printed out for her during those summer months. Everyone else was on email, which is how we communicated with potential attendees. Mom didn't have a computer but

I wanted her to keep up to date on what was happening. For the Events, I printed her out the invitation and a bio of the speaker. She keeps every piece of paper and, though I used to complain about that, now I'm glad.

Some of the recipes in my little spiral notebook i.e. cookbook had notations such as: "I made this when Carol Bush came because I knew she'd like it" or "made this because I have enough zucchini to feed an army." I'd made many of my recipes based on who was coming and what I thought would work for that particular group of attendees. Of course, what was ripe and delicious in the garden at that particular moment was the most important factor.

This is also when I really got into cooking. The vegetables were so fresh and mind-bendingly delicious that cooking was a gift from heaven.

Each summer, I also grew herbs: rosemary, basil, sage, parsley, thyme, oregano, lavender, mint, and a few others. I used them copiously in everything I made. I also made flower arrangements with them and gave pots and pots of herbs away.

After a while people started avoiding me when the garden was in full bloom. Not really. But it does bring to mind that old joke: Do you know why southerners lock their cars when they go to Church in summer? Because, if you leave your doors unlocked, when you come out of church your car is full of zucchini.

It is a prolific vegetable.

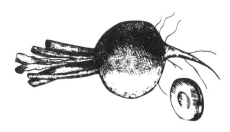

You Never Know, Do You?

Sweet Beets

I met Gillian Spencer in New York City. She was referred to me by a friend from Virginia Beach. She came to my office at 52nd and Broadway; we talked for a bit about a potential book she wanted to write on healing. Then we walked around the corner to the local French Bistro. She moved the chairs around to make sure she sat with her back to the diners as I sat against the wall. This was all outside on Seventh Avenue at the corner of 53rd Street.

Not long after we'd been chatting, I noticed a few young women around us start to point and whisper to each other. I wondered what was going on and kept glancing around to see who they were talking about. It seemed to me they were pointing at Gillian but for the life of me I couldn't figure out why that would be.

A young woman came over, knelt down by Gillian's chair and quietly asked, "Are you Daisy?"

Gillian, ever gracious I found out later, said, "I play Daisy, but I'm Gillian Spencer." And just like that a line formed and she was signing autographs. Heavens.

We went back to my office and she told me who she WAS. Gillian Spencer was an actress in soap operas and a writer of soap operas. She'd started out on *The Secret Storm*, then *The Edge of Night*, *Guiding Light*, and *One Life to Live* but the reason she was recognized that day at lunch was because of *All My Children*, where she played Daisy Cortland, Palmer's first wife. It was a 20 year role where she died several times but magically came back to life and started all over. It was soap opera at its best.

Wherever we went this happened. She said she truly loved her fans. They were so devoted to their soaps and appreciated the characters, with all of their foibles and graces.

Gillian had come to talk about a potential book based on her psychic and healing experiences. Included would be the readings she'd given to doctors, researchers and interested seekers. She had an extraordinary archive of readings that addressed many issues we're dealing with today and many of her readings were given 20 to 30 years ago. She predicted the future; a future that we are living now.

On October 20, 2007 Gillian gave an excellent presentation. It was titled: *Intimate Connections: Earth, the Universe and Us*. In it she shared some of her personal stories and her view of the interconnectedness as it manifests from the single cell, to the body, to Earth and out into the Cosmos. It was a message of love and science in which connectedness was repeated in many ways. Its message was that "the family of Earth" is reconnecting with families in the "everywhere." It is a link that makes all of Nature and Cosmos wonderfully personal, not separate, but an intrinsic part of who and what we are.

We had an experiential session where we explored contemplative music as a pathway that brought us deeper into ourselves and into greater contact with each other, the earth and the universe.

In 2006, Gillian moved from New York City to Virginia Beach in order to devote her time to lecturing, and continuing her health/life readings for interested individuals.

Gillian is an extraordinarily talented woman at every single thing she does. We were blessed to have her come and speak to us.

This recipe just makes me feel good, like Gillian does. And she loves my beets.

Pickled Beets

In my garden I grow beets because I love beets. As a child my Mom told me if I ate my beets, they'd make me pretty. An extra gift from the Beet Goddesses because, truth was, I was just happy to eat them. You'll need 8 six-ounce jars.

10–12 medium beets, washed
Water
3 cups white vinegar
$\frac{1}{2}$ cup sugar
1 tablespoon allspice
12 black peppercorns
1 clove garlic

1. Bring a large pot of water to boil and add the scrubbed beets. Decrease the heat to a simmer and cook for about 45 minutes, or until the beets are fork-tender.
2. While the beets cook, prepare and sterilize 8 6 oz jars.
3. Pour water off the beets and after they cool a bit, peel and slice them.
4. Make the pickling mixture in a medium sized pan. Add the vinegar, sugar, allspice, pepper and garlic. Once the mixture comes to a boil, cut it back to medium and simmer for 5 minutes.
5. Put the sliced beets into the sterilized jar, leaving about a $\frac{1}{2}$ at the top. Strain out spices and pour over the sliced beets in the jars.
6. Seal the jars.

You'll have beets all winter!

Ghosts

Virginia Beach Chili

L isa was giving a talk at the Hanover Book Festival in July of 2008. Hanover has a long history promoting writers of history and inspiring avid readers. I went along for moral support although she needed none. She was in her element giving advice for want-to-be writers and writers who were trying to get the attention of an agent. She gave a two-hour workshop on how to write a book proposal while I manned the table of books she'd brought to sell.

Right across from where I was sitting was a young, vibrant woman. She was slim, with bright red lipstick and gorgeous red hair. She was in sell mode and, unlike me, she was selling books. I wondered what her book was about but with all the people milling about and talking, I couldn't really hear her sales pitch. She was energetic and engaging and I could see each time she leaned over the table to talk to someone that between her sandal and Capri pants, she had bright tattoos. The bottom one looked like a TV set. One of the old ones with antennas. I could not figure out why this young lady would have TVs tattooed on her leg. And I am one curious person-anyone who knows me at all will tell you that.

Eventually curiosity got the best of me and I stepped around my table and walked to hers.

I listened while she told a young man about her newest book. She explained, "As founder of the Virginia Society of Paranormal Education and Research I'd heard talk and rumors about hauntings at several famous Virginia landmarks. I decided to investigate and, from the data that I discovered during my investigations, I wrote *Haunted Battlefields: Virginia Civil War Ghosts*."

Opening the book, she pointed out several photos, explaining that she'd found evidence about all sorts of mysteries, that could determine who still roams the grounds of Berkeley Plantation; if spectral children play and frolic during the night at Richmond's Edgar Allen Poe Museum; if the restless souls who perished in a theater fire trip the alarms at Monumental Church; and if ghostly battles continue at Sailor's Creek and Cold Harbor.

Well, who wouldn't be captivated by that?

He purchased the book and I moved forward and asked her if I could see the tattoo on her leg. It was so out of context that she gave me a look, *who are you lady and why do you want to look at my tattoo*? It was a decision for her, since I hadn't mentioned buying a book, and there was a line behind me of people with money in hand.

I was smiling and not forthcoming so making a quick decision she politely said, "When I'm done with this line I'll come over to your booth and show you."

And she did. From her ankle past her knee she had tattoos of television sets. At her ankle it started off with really old versions up to the newest type of televisions. I asked her why and what she said was astounding to me because it seemed so completely obvious, true and powerful. Television was the modern totem, the modern story teller and the modern fire we all sit around to listen for wisdom. Or not. She was wise far beyond her years. I'd thought she was maybe 18 or 20 but I found out she was a married woman with children! Naturally, I asked Beth Brown if she'd come and give a talk to our Dairy Barn Group. She immediately said yes. Nice.

Beth Brown describes herself (from her website) as a connoisseur of freckled faces, carnival sideshows, and dry wit. Her creative career began not with writing, but with visual art and illustration. This probably explains why she still prefers to write with a paper and pen.

Beth turned her focus toward words after learning that the history and legends she had been researching as a hobby were quickly slipping away with the previous generation. Her non-fiction books became a mission to preserve the events of the past while making them fun and entertaining for modern readers. She made the transition to fiction in 2013 with *Underground*, an urban fantasy for middle-grade readers that carefully weaves true historical events with action and adventure.

She was so busy that November was her first opportunity to drive down to make a presentation. She was entertaining, knowledgeable and seriously funny. We heard stories about historical ghosts of Richmond and the surrounding areas. And watched video clips she'd made of ghostly sightings. Yikes.

In Virginia Beach, a friend made the best and the hottest chili I ever had. I asked for the recipe over and over but she always said no; it was just hers and she didn't want to share it. Finally, after I stopped asking, she gave it to me as a birthday present, all wrapped up and on special birthday paper.

November 2008: It was a chilly day so we had hot Chili. I've always like food that made tears run, cleared my sinuses and woke up my taste buds. This chili filled the bill.

Virginia Beach Chili

(When cleaning jalapenos, you may want to wear kitchen gloves or cut the peppers under running tap water. Be careful not to touch your eyes when working with them.)

A large pot
Vegetable oil for cooking
2 large onions, coarsely chopped
1½ pounds ground beef
4 cloves garlic, minced
1 6oz can tomato paste
1 15oz can red kidney beans
2 cups tomato juice
7 drops Tabasco
2 tablespoons chili powder
1–2 jalapeno peppers, seeds cleaned, and cut into 10
    slices

1. Pour the oil into the base of the large pot and heat over high. Once hot, add the onions, beef and garlic. Stir constantly, breaking apart the meat and browning it. The onions and garlic should be soft and translucent.
2. Add all at once the tomato paste, kidney beans, tomato juice, Tabasco, chili powder and jalapeno slices.
3. Cook over medium heat for 2 hours, stirring occasionally.
4. Serve with rice or heavy bread slices because it is very spicy.

Serves 6.

The Sacred Feminine
Zucchini

A client of Lisa's, Lynda Terry had a new book, *The 11 Intentions: Invoking the Sacred Feminine as a Pathway to Inner Peace*. We thought that sounded great so we invited her to speak. She came in April of 2007 and talked about why the Women-Peace-Sacred Feminine connection is essential for attaining individual and collective peace. She led us in a guided meditation and taught us methods to be peaceful within ourselves. These are processes that as we practice them, will help the world around us to be a more peaceful place.

Lynda Terry is a meditation teacher, author and founder of Vessels of Peace. She began teaching meditation in the early 1990s and after her own meditation practice—initiated to cope with a life crisis—transformed her physically, emotionally and spiritually. She had found her calling.

Lynda has a master's degree from Gannon University and has completed professional and advanced training programs with the Center for Mind-Body Medicine in Washington, D.C.

As you can imagine, in my garden whenever I grew zucchini plants I had too much zucchini and gave lots away and made lots of variations on anything zucchini. One recipe everyone loved was my take on Paula Deen's recipe for Zucchini Bread. Other zucchini recipes follow. I had a lot of zucchini.

Zucchini Bread

Makes two loaves.

3¼ cups all-purpose flour

1½ teaspoons salt

1 teaspoon nutmeg

2 teaspoons baking soda

1 teaspoon ground cinnamon

3 cups sugar

1 cup vegetable oil

4 eggs

⅓ cup water

2 cups grated zucchini

1 cup chopped walnuts

1. Preheat oven to 350 degrees.
2. In a large bowl combine flour, salt, nutmeg, baking soda, cinnamon and sugar. Mix.
3. In a separate bowl, beat together the oil, eggs, and water. Add the zucchini.
4. Mix wet and dry ingredients, adding nuts at the end.
5. Bake in 2 standard prepared loaf pans, (butter and flour the pan) for one hour or until a toothpick comes out clean.

Zucchini Frittata

Many of the speakers spent the weekend with me and I'd make vegetable frittatas and serve them for breakfast. They were always a hit.

1 zucchini, sliced
1 small onion, sliced
1 tablespoon butter
1 tablespoon olive oil plus more to coat pan
2–3 small potatoes
6–8 egg
$\frac{1}{2}$ cup grated Parmesan cheese
$\frac{1}{2}$ cup cream or half-and-half
Salt and pepper to taste

1. In a large, heavy-bottomed fry pan, melt the butter and oil.
2. Add the zucchini and onion and sauté until tender. Remove to a bowl.
3. While they cook, pop two or three small potatoes into the microwave for a few minutes to soften them. Alternatively, if you don't have a microwave, parboil the potatoes in heavily salted water for about 10 minutes. The potatoes should be a bit soft.
4. Add enough olive oil to coat the fry pan. Slice the potatoes to cover the bottom of the oven-proof skillet.
5. Beat 6 to 8 eggs with one-half the Parmesan cheese. Add the cream or half-and-half—whichever works for you. Add the salt and pepper to taste.
6. Cook the first layer of potatoes over medium high heat for about 5 minutes so they develop a hard crust.
7. Spread the zucchini and onion mix over the potatoes and let that cook for 2–3 minutes.

8. Finally pour the egg mixture on top and let it set over the medium high heat for about 5 minutes.
9. Take the oven-proof pan and put it in the oven at 350 degrees for about 15 minutes to cook through.
10. When it is done, take the pan out and spread the remaining parmesan on top of the frittata. Put the pan under the broiler for a few moments, watching constantly, until the cheese is sizzling and done.
11. Take out and let sit for another 10 minutes, then slice like a pizza (a pizza cutter is perfect for cutting it).

Serves 4.

Zucchini and Other Vegetables, Steamed

1 cup each of sliced zucchini, yellow squash and eggplant
1 small onion, sliced
1/2 cup olive oil
Large handful of herbs such as basil,
     parsley and rosemary
Salt and pepper to taste

1. Steam the zucchini, yellow squash, and eggplant onion quickly, and transfer to bowl.
2. While steaming, mix the olive oil, herbs (basil, parsley, rosemary) salt and pepper. Pour over the vegetables and toss.

Serves 4.

Summer of 2006: An Interlude
Tabouli

Even as the garden called to me and I was answering, I was still traveling to Manhattan, the publishing hub of the universe, for my Paraview Pocket Books imprint. This chapter tells the story of one trip during 2006. It'll give a feel for the differences between my country life and my city life. Looking back I realize I was having the best of both worlds.

For two weeks that summer I was in New York staying at the Westside apartment of my phenomenal actress and psychic friend Gillian Spencer. She lived in one of those huge apartment buildings with TRUMP plastered across the top, down by the Hudson River. She was away and I was taking care of her son's dog, Dennis. Her son had passed away and she'd taken in Dennis. Doggy care; this was a first for me. Dennis was very sweet but old and incontinent. We took a lot of walks.

After planting vegetables and flowers and hosting a Dairy Barn Event, I'd taken a train to New York. Richmond, Virginia has the best train service, a straight door-to-door trip leaving at 8 AM and arriving at Penn Station in NYC at 2 PM As usual when I was in the city it was a super busy time; packed with meetings, dinners with friends, attending lectures and talking to clients.

Dennis didn't bark but he stared effectively. I'd wake up in the mornings and Dennis would be staring at me, dead in the eye. I'd jump up, throw my clothes on and out we'd go. He knew all the dogs we'd meet and they knew him.

"Good Morning Dennis" I'd hear throughout our 20 to 30 minute stroll through the park in front of the building. I'd just smile. Then we'd sit in the sun and enjoy a new day. It was a good way to start in New York City.

I'd always subscribed to *New York Magazine.* I love magazines and read a variety; from *Archeology* to *Cowboys and Indians* (all my lady-friends wanted to look at the cowboy pictures!), to *Vanity Fair, Architectural Digest, Veranda,* and *Vogue.* Plus my favorites, *Spirituality and Health* and the A.R.E.'s *Venture Inward.* Now everything is on-line but I still like to hold a magazine and flip through the pages. *New York Magazine* had the scoop on new art exhibits, new restaurants, new Broadway shows and before every trip north, I'd make a list.

A French country restaurant had opened at 79th and Amsterdam and it was on my list. I scheduled a dinner at Nice Matin with Emily Squires. Emily was one of my dearest friends, soul sister and supporter when times were tough. *New York Magazine* had said: crowded, loud and great food. It was all three. We talked for hours catching each other up on what was going on in our separate worlds.

Emily and I attended a party for parapsychologist, physicist and laser scientist, Russell Targ. He'd given a talk at FIONS the day before I'd arrived in NYC. The party was given by Annemarie Colbin, the author of *Food and Healing.* Annemarie founded The Natural Gourmet Institute for Health and Culinary Arts in 1977. She was all about natural food before it became trendy. Eventually Annemarie also became a FIONS Board member and the quality of our dinner parties and cocktail parties for speakers really moved up a notch.

Russell was tall, slender, with coke bottle glasses. Originally a physicist and laser scientist, he was one of the first to work on the

Remote Viewing Program at Stanford Research Institute in Palo Alto, California. Hal Puthoff, a physicist was the original developer of remote viewing and he was a savvy politician, as well as an extraordinary research scientist.

I liked and admired Hal from the moment I met him in the mid-80s. We were having lunch at a hotel where we were both attending a parapsychology conference in Boulder, Colorado. He was animated and articulate and shorter and rounder but cuter than Russell. He was explaining to me about physics and how much energy there was in just one little square inch of air/space. He loved his work so much and loved physics so much that he could barely stay in his seat. It was an invigorating, joyous lunch conversation.

In 1977, they had written a book titled, *Mind-Reach: Scientists Look at Psychic Abilities*. It was the book that led to the US Army's psychic spy program and the development of remote viewing.

The party was fun, reconnecting with old friends and meeting new ones. Talking business.

On Saturday night I was having dinner with another writer friend, Marianne. I'd suggested a place near her on my NY Magazine list and she was up for it. We met through my literary agency. She was a freelance writer, a ghost-writer and "connected" to the zeitgeist of New York City. When I got to her apartment, she said her neighbors were chefs for *Gourmet Magazine*. They'd just brought over a meal made in their test kitchen. We ditched the new restaurant idea. Their meal was delicious.

Afterwards we walked to the Trestle Restaurant and Bar on 10th Avenue because Marianne wanted me to meet a couple who were making Bollywood Films. They were high energy, expanded by 20, and talked about the excitement of the Indian film industry enthusiastically and loudly. Their new film was premiering in a month. I was relieved when we stepped out of the bar since my ears were ringing. The farm was nice for my sensitive hearing. New York had always been really loud and full of really loud people screaming at each other in order to be heard over the traffic, street noise and other people. I liked the peace and quiet of Bracey and the farm.

But, this being New York nightlife, after having dinner at Marianne's apartment thanks to *Gourmet* magazine, drinks at The Trestle and learning about Bollywood, we hopped into a taxi and crossed town to visit a Shaman.

In the taxi we discussed a client of mine from the 90s. Marianne and I had bonded because years before, I'd taken her with me to Kennebunkport, Maine, to meet with a high ranking Army officer who wanted to write a book about psychic research around the world, which he knew intimately, having been involved and at one point as overseer of the remote viewing program for the U. S Army. He'd retired and wanted to write. He eventually decided to fictionalize his book which I think was an excellent idea. He was a grand, gruff, quiet man of huge gravitas with a talkative, gracious, perfect Army wife. After his wife went to bed, we sat drinking scotch and he talked. I wish I could've recorded our conversations with this man but he wouldn't allow it. Even though it was years ago, that was a weekend Marianne and I would never forget.

The Shaman lived in a penthouse and had huge trees growing on his roof. We drank wine and enjoyed the view of Manhattan rooftops. We also looked at the moon through his telescope. We had a fascinating conversation about Shamanism. He was in his 70s, had a scruffy wild-eyed-been-everywhere-seen-everything look. I thought maybe he'd had too much Ayahuasca. He'd traveled the world; been through shamanic rituals with many tribes along the Amazon, as well as traveled to Mongolia, Brazil, and said, he'd even spent time with Native tribes in Canada.

I got back to Gillian's apartment at 2 AM and hustled Dennis out for a quick walk and tinkle. That was Saturday night.

On Sunday I rested.

Monday, I had a meeting at Simon and Schuster. The editor-in-chief of Paraview Pocket Books was Patrick Huyghe and the publisher of Pocket Books was the perceptive and savvy Louise

Burk. Our list was doing well and we were looking forward to publishing more books. Publishing was going through an extraordinary upheaval. Barnes and Noble Bookstores had been busy putting most small bookstores out of business, and we had discovered that those small bookstores were the ones that mostly sold books in our genre. Meanwhile, Amazon was squeezing Barnes and Noble. It was a time of change for all of publishing.

We discussed marketing our published books and ideas for new books we'd like to publish. We'd started with Loren Coleman's *Mysterious America: The Ultimate Guide to the Nation's Weirdest Wonders, Strangest Spots, and Creepiest Creatures* and *The Copycat Effect: How the Media and Popular Culture Trigger the Mayhem in Tomorrow's Headlines*. Nick Redfern wrote *Three Men Seeking Monsters* for us. Followed up with Dean Radin's book, *Entangled Minds: Extrasensory Experiences in a Quantum Reality* and Lyn Buchanan's *The Seventh Sense; The Secrets of Remote Viewing As Told By A 'Psychic Spy' For The U.S. Military.*

We published a book out of our genre but which we were really excited about. It was titled, *Men in Black Dresses: A Quest for the Future Among Wisdom-Makers of the Middle East* by anthropologist Yvonne Seng. I had serious interest in this book from TV producers. It was perfect format for a series but it never happened. It still could, who knows?

I had been asked to give a talk about publishing and the life of a literary agent in Manhattan at the Virginia Festival of the Book to be held in Charlottesville, Virginia the following spring. Louise was very enthusiastic about that. I was too.

Patrick was a well-respected editor with massive knowledge in the genre, formidable contacts and had written many books on various subjects as well as cryptozoology and UFO books. He fit in perfectly with our imprint at S&S for Paraview Pocket Books. We were lucky to get him. He now has his own publishing company and a website, Anomalist.com.

Later that week I spent time with Jessie, an artist whose apartment overlooked Gramercy Park, which she was always painting. Jessie is a professional artist. She was born in New York City and loved it there. Multi-talented, she has been an art director and production designer for theater sets, advertising and music videos. She was all New York. I met her when my friend, the actor Roy Thinnes, introduced us. After starting out acting in *General Hospital*, he moved to films and at that time he had a recurring role in the TV series, *X-Files*. He was dating Jessie.

I also had lunch at the Princeton Club with an old friend. While waiting for him, I listened as a marketing guy from FOX News went on about how their viewers wanted "red meat" and he didn't care if they were real facts or not; they were angry old men and they wanted red meat. He kept saying that phrase. It was unsettling, to say the least. From the expression on the face of the man he was talking to, he was taken aback as well. It was a strange conversation for the staid and scholarly Princeton crowd.

I was grateful when my friend arrived and we talked about his children and my children. We were the same age, divorced and interested in spirituality. Years before, we'd dated. He was as good-hearted a man as I've ever met.

I had many more meetings with clients. As well as dinners, foreign films, movies that'd never make it out of Manhattan and the theater with friends. Although it was an extremely rewarding and entertaining time in New York City, it was time to go home. It was always a long train ride home, lots of stops to allow freight trains to pass, while we sat on the sideline which was contrary to the ride to New York City. I never figured that out.

Back in Bracey, I found an invitation to a party from a friend I'd grown up with. Faye was a trim, fun, worldly-wise, witty and a take charge and make things happen kind of person. I'd told her that most of the people I'd grown up with were exactly as I left them, and as nice as they were, we had very little in common. In fact, they seemed angry that I'd left and if I said anything about my life they thought I was bragging, when in fact I was relating my real life experiences and I wasn't bragging at all. I mean, I was a southern woman and southern women don't brag. Faye said, "I know who you need to meet and I'll put together a group for a party." That sounded good to me although I thought I knew all the people in the area interested in consciousness, holistic healing and spirituality. I was wrong.

The garden called and I weeded, harvested and cooked. It was all that I wanted. Everyone joked that whenever you wanted Sandra you just had to go to the garden and there she'd be. That was true.

Finally Faye's party day came and my Mom and I drove over to her house on the Lake. The yard was beautifully designed and perfectly landscaped. My yard and garden were always in disarray because I was always changing things, planting new things, and digging up old plants to move them here and there. Faye's yard was my fantasy garden. The house was high on a cliff and the landscape was designed to show off the yard and the view of Lake Gaston. Organized, neat, well-designed and with the backdrop blue of the Lake it was right out of a magazine.

Faye had gathered a group of people who were interested in the same things I was interested in, namely consciousness and deep spirituality. Faye is a true friend and a great party giver.

Faye's friends became my new friends almost immediately. They included her neighbors who'd recently moved from Richmond and were great Caroline Myss book-readers and Unity Church goers, a friend of Mom's brought her daughter who'd just moved in to help take care of her and was interested in our genre, and a couple who'd recently moved from San Jose, California who said they'd had too many psychic experiences to go into it. No party at the Lake would be complete without a real estate agent. This one was from nearby Roanoke Rapids and she was very serious, notifying us, "I am on the path." She also said she had a flat in Paris; her get-away place from the Lake. My. Now that was impressive.

The woman from San Jose said they'd been flying-in healers and, as we were chatting, she casually commented, "I see your aura; all reds and golds." She'd bought and re-stored a house built in 1774. And those were just a few of the new friends that Faye had gathered. It was an amazing party.

A few weeks after I returned from New York, Jessie, my artist friend from New York, called to tell me a funny story. She was out on the street in front of her apartment building painting Gramercy Park all in bloom when she saw someone walk by that she'd met at a party of mine a few years before. Daryl was easy to remember because he was so doggone handsome. He was an artist from Richmond, a sculptor. To make extra money, he modeled. He'd been teaching at VCU but decided if he was going to make it he had to move to NYC. So he did. My daughter babysat his kids when she was a teenager. We re-connected. Ladies really loved him; but what's not to love? Handsome, charming, sexy and artsy.

Jessie was reminding him that she'd met him at a party of mine and they were chatting when another friend of Jessie's came up to say hello. It was the actress Julia Roberts and her husband, Danny Moder. Introductions were given all around and when my name came up, Julia said, "Oh, I know who she is." Jessie and Daryl looked at her in surprise. Julia told them that she had been considering a project from one of my clients. Julia was reading the manuscript about a famous western cowgirl barrel racer and her horse. They stood there chatting about the amazing three-way connection and the common thread was Sandra Martin. And yes, as well as books on consciousness and spirituality, I sold cowboy and cowgirl books, too.

My garden flourished while I was away. I had a huge amount of parsley. It was eat-me green and luscious looking. In the past I had used parsley as a garnish or in soups and salads. Only after I had a Tabouli salad at a restaurant in Raleigh did I start to use lots of it. This is as close as I could come to their recipe and I make it often now.

Tabouli or is it Tabbouleh?
A Lebanese Dish

Traditionally bulgur is used but I use whatever grain I have in the pantry: sometimes it is quinoa, sometimes amaranth, sometimes plain old white rice.

2 cups finely chopped parsley
1 large tomato, seeded and chopped
1 cup bulgur or grain of your choice, cooked according to
    package directions
1 garlic clove, minced
2 spring onions, finely sliced
½ cup chopped fresh mint
Fresh lemon juice to taste
Olive oil to taste
Salt to taste
Pinch of allspice, pepper, or ginger (optional)

In a large bowl, combine all the ingredients, tasting as you go.

Serve.

Governing Insights
Pesto

On June 16, 2007, Sylvia Clute spoke at the Dairy Barn. The previous month, I had attended an author event at the Brunswick Library in nearby Lawrenceville, Virginia. I was wandering around and Sylvia's energy just drew me. Somehow I knew that she had something to say that I wanted to hear, and after hearing her, I knew I had to share it with others. Sylvia has a gentle but determined spirit which makes her a thoughtful and insightful lawyer. She also studied the *Course in Miracles*.

She had written a compelling and unusual novel with a much needed message.

The novel, *Destiny Unveiled: Seven Spiritual Principles for Governing a People* tells the story of attorney Christi Daniel as she searches for better answers to our legal, governmental, and political systems. Her mentor through this process is our Founding Father and first President of the United States of America, George Washington. Speaking to her through the ages, he reveals to Christi a master plan of seven steps to create a world in which harmony, balance and unity can save us from disaster.

Her latest book, *Beyond Vengeance, Beyond Duality* offers readers a blueprint, a hands-on way for transformative change that begins with a central pillar of our culture, how we define justice. The unique way in which the pieces of the puzzle are assembled in *Beyond Vengeance, Beyond Duality* make it more difficult for those who defend the old order to make their case, and gives legitimacy to those who are building the new forms. Through this frame, old approaches to law, government, business, religion, education and economics are seen in a fresh new way that leads to concrete answers. A new world is at hand and we need not wait!

In her lecture to us, she took us through steps to a unified approach to law, government and social order based on the crucial distinction between love and fear. The key, she said, is being able to distinguish between punitive and unitive justice. When we understand this distinction, our world of greed, violence and war in the midst of breathtaking acts of love, kindness and generosity makes perfect sense. As we analyze the two systems we discover that punitive justice reflects a dualistic way of thinking that makes the "us versus them" dichotomy seem reasonable. Her theory of unitive justice recognizes the interconnectedness of all that is— that is that what we do to others, we do to ourselves.

Sylvia is currently head of the Alliance for Unitive Justice at Virginia Union University in Richmond, Virginia. Before that, she was a trial attorney in private practice in Richmond, VA. She holds an MA in Public Administration from the Kennedy School of Government at Harvard University, a *Juris Doctor* from Boston University School of Law, an MA in Public Administration from the University of California at Berkeley, and a BA in Political Science from the University of Colorado.

Sylvia was so inspiring and awesomely brilliant, we had her speak twice.

Somehow every summer I grow too much basil. It just runs wild on me. I started out years ago with a few seeds and grew six plants and now, every year, I have a big crop of 20 or more plants. All volunteers. I give lots away, make dozens of fresh tomato, basil and mozzarella salads and, best of all, I make and freeze pesto. The bright green flavor of delicious basil brings summer into any winter meal. I love pesto and use it in many ways: stuffed into chicken breasts, spread on a tomato and cheese sandwich, and of course, it pairs naturally with many pasta and fish dishes.

Pesto

2 cups fresh basil leaves, washed and dried

1/2 cup parsley, washed and dried (optional)

1 teaspoon salt

1 teaspoon pepper

2 large cloves garlic, cut up

1/2 cup olive oil

1/4 cup walnuts or pine nuts

1/2 cup grated Parmesan or Romano cheese

1. Using a food processer, put the nuts, basil, parsley, salt, pepper, garlic, olive oil, and bowl. Process until completely combined and smooth.
2. Add parmesan cheese at the end.
3. Transfer to a storage bowl, preferably with a lid, and use in whatever way you choose. Always bring to room temperature before using.

Serve.

Seeking Men in Black Dresses
Cucumber Recipes

In August of 2005, Yvonne Seng gave a presentation at The Dairy Barn. Years before Yvonne had submitted her manuscript to me while I was still an agent in New York City. I was so moved, inspired, and excited about this manuscript which became the book entitled *Men in Black Dresses*, that I called her up and the next day took a train to Alexandria, Virginia to meet her. I loved her energy, her courage and her super smarts. She was an extraordinary writer and I wanted to represent her.

We met in Alexandria's Old Towne. We had an extremely long, deliciously rich conversation, and I was wowed.

Yvonne told me that the manuscript which I'd loved, *Men In Black Dresses: A Quest for the Future Among Wisdom-Makers in the Middle East* came about from a chance meeting fifteen years before. She'd met a charismatic holy man on a train trip to Upper Egypt. He turned out to be the venerable Catholic Bishop of Asyout. Mysteriously, she said, not sure why, but she promised him she'd return one day. He said if she came back she'd see the future. Fifteen years passed. She woke up in a cold sweat in her Washington D.C. home and had a vision. In her vision she was being summoned to return to the Middle East to find that holy man. The manuscript was about her journey back.

The story is full of mishaps and adventures as Yvonne wheedles her way into places no woman is allowed, ultimately meeting spiritual leaders on the top of mountains under moonlight. Her interviews and encounters with religious visionaries detail how these holy men yearn for peace, the right planetary stewardships and respect for wisdom.

Yvonne was a natural storyteller and a deep spiritual seeker. She is also an achiever. As a cultural historian specializing in the Middle East and Turkey she has taught courses on peace studies at American University's Center for Global Peace, and on religion, history, and Islamic culture at Georgetown and Princeton Universities and Wesley Theological Seminary. Born in Australia, she has worked and traveled widely in the Middle East.

I published Yvonne's manuscript, *Men In Black Dresses: A Quest for the Future Among Wisdom-Makers in the Middle East* under my Paraview publishing imprint.

Yvonne loved our fresh-off-the-vine cucumbers. Following are a couple of recipes.

Don't go for the really big cucumbers because they have much less flavor. It was one of the strangest things I observed when I moved to the city. When my friends were buying vegetables they always picked the largest ones—more vegetable for their money I'd guess. I always got the smaller ones, if available. The large ones didn't have much flavor while the smaller ones were full of flavor.

Cucumbers the Southern Way #1

3–4 medium-sized cucumbers

Salt to taste

5–6 tablespoons vinegar or to taste.

1. Peel and slice them into ¼ to ⅓ inch rounds and put them in ice water to cover adding salt and vinegar.
2. Serve immediately.

Cucumbers #2

3–4 medium sized cucumbers—seed if the cucumbers
   are large, peel if needed

1 small onion, sliced thin

Sour cream to cover

Salt and pepper to taste

2–3 tablespoons chopped dill to taste (optional)

1. Slice the cucumbers.
2. Slice small onion, and put them into a bowl.
3. Sour cream to cover.
4. Salt and pepper as needed.
5. Dill if you like that flavor.
6. Mix all ingredients together and chill.

This is good sauce for salmon or any kind of fish.

Old Friends
Squash Casserole

Cynthia McTyre is one of my mother's dearest friends and now is one of mine, too. We've become fast friends since I moved back.

Cynthia is one of those mostly-quiet southern women with mostly unspoken but extremely strong opinions; opinions that always surprise me in a really good way. She has eclectic taste; she loves old time music, loves modern folk/country, and is an avid Facebooker. She keeps us in touch with everything we need to know.

When she was living in Durham, North Carolina, she worked as a secretary for Dr. J. B. Rhine. Dr Rhine coined the phrase ESP: Extra-Sensory Perception.

Cynthia gave one of our first talks at the Dairy Barn. It was on EFT, the Emotional Freedom Technique. We'd never heard of it until she gave us the basics and taught us how to do it. A year or so later, Dr. Larry Burk updated us on the research and new techniques.

EFT is based on the acupuncture model of energy healing. Research has found that tapping on energy meridians works on emotional issues as well as physical ones. It is a simple, effective technique based on tapping parts of the face, neck and upper body with your fingertips while repeating a carefully-worded message to acknowledge and heal a seeker's problem.

Cynthia loves squash. My Mom loves squash. I love squash. We like it made the old-fashioned way with brown sugar. We also love casseroles for Sunday dinners.

Squash, Southern-Style

I loved squash as a kid and have made it all my life. When you grow it, you grow a lot of it. One plant and I have enough for the summer and the freezer.

4–5 medium-sized squash cut into ¼ inch slices

2 medium onions, sliced

Oil for cooking

½ cup brown sugar

Add salt and pepper to taste.

1. In a large fry pan over high heat, add the oil.
2. Put the onion in and cook until tender.
3. Add all of the squash. Stir and cover the pan to let them steam, opening the pot and mashing with a fork or breaking the vegetables apart from time to time.
4. When the vegetables are completely soft and cooked through, add the sugar, salt and pepper.
5. Cook, uncovered, until the sugar and spice integrates into the dish, approximately 3–5 minutes.

Serve.

Squash Casserole

You'll need 9 x 13 Pyrex or oven-safe casserole for this dish.

4 cups sliced yellow squash

½ cup chopped onion

Oil for cooking

35 buttery round crackers, crushed

1 cup shredded cheddar cheese

2 eggs, slightly beaten

¾ cup milk

¼ cup butter, melted

1 teaspoon salt

Black pepper to taste

1. In a large oiled skillet over medium heat, add the squash and onion. Pour in small amount of water, cover and cook until tender. 7 to 10 minutes. Drain well and place in a large bowl.
2. In another bowl, mix together cracker crumbs and cheese; stir ½ of the cracker mixture with the squash mixture. Stir in the beaten eggs, melted butter, salt and pepper.
3. Spread into a 9 x 13 baking dish.
4. Sprinkle top with remaining cracker mixture and dot with two tablespoons of butter.
5. Bake in a 350 degree preheated oven for 25 minutes or until top is slightly brown.

Serves 6.

Little Green Men
Chicken Salad

In addition to cultivating the vegetable patch, I also worked in my flower garden at my home, which was about a mile from the Dairy Barn, up a dirt road.

Right by my home driveway was a barren, rain washed hill without much vegetation. I thought it needed some love or, at the very least, some improvement. I first dug a small garden near the walkway to the back door. I planted variegated green and blue-green hostas there because it was under the shade of several big oak trees. I dug a curvy furrow from the hosta bed down the hill about 20 feet. I walked around the farm fields and picked up rocks to build a little retaining wall. I knew that if I didn't build a retaining wall the rains would come and push my carefully dug up and composted beautiful, raw, virginal dirt right down the hill and into the lake. The rocks worked perfectly.

I planted lavender and pink Rose of Sharon along that wall as well as petunias, and whatever package of flower seeds I happened to see at the Dollar Store. I also planted purple foxglove in honor of my Dad who survived his heart disease so many years thanks to the digitalis derived from foxglove, as I've said before.

Each spring I dug out more of the hill and built more rock walls. I bought and planted hydrangeas, holly bushes and shrubs; so many shrubs that I've forgotten their names. I dug up starter plants from friends' yards, old plants like nandinas and the ubiquitous purple iris. At garden centers, I almost always purchased the dry, sad and barely-alive potted plants. The ones that looked like they were on their last legs were the ones with my name on them. I felt sorry for them in the nurseries.

The hill started to bloom and be a joyous, happy garden. It glowed. Lilac bushes near the walkway to the back door always smelled so heavenly in the summer. In every season, friends wanted to walk through my garden when they came to visit. Eventually, my nephew helped me to build a water garden and place heavy flat rocks around it. It was beautiful.

Often, when I was in my garden, which was a lot, when I wasn't traveling or working on the Dairy Barn, I wondered about fairy people, leprechauns, and elves. Were they real? I'd sing to them. I'd ask them to show themselves. I felt their energy. The garden was a magical place. I painted a big sign that I nailed to the garden shed: The Fairy Garden. But I saw no fairies.

After working in the garden I often went upstairs to sit and read. Or work on a proposal. Mental stimulation after all the physical work.

Visitors often commented that my house was a terrarium. I had trees I'd moved around for 20 years. I had a jade tree that was almost four feet tall, a gorgeous plant, and it was always in my bedroom in a place of honor, with perfect lighting, because it was a sensitive spirit. Naturally, I talked to all my plants because they were old friends.

On this particular day, I was hot and tired and I had a fan blowing on me while I was reading. I was sitting in my comfy chair by my jade tree happy as could be. Not thinking anything special, not sleepy, nor anxious, just even-keeled, with book in hand. I thought I saw movement out of the corner of my eye and turned to the jade plant. And there looking right at me was a leprechaun. He was right out of central casting. He was sitting easy as pie on a nice fat limb of the jade tree, one foot up, elbow on his knee and just smiling at me. Green clothes, cute face, smiling twinkly eyes and he looked at me as if to say, "Oh, so you can see me now?" I was amazed, awed and excited, all at once. I just stared. Not saying a word out loud but thanking him in my mind over and over for showing himself.

After a short while he just started to fade away until he had disappeared altogether. I smiled and gave a thankful prayer for that beautiful gift.

I loved my herbs and used one or more in almost every dish. Chicken salad was always a big winner for Events at the Dairy Barn because I loaded it up with all sorts of herbs. And I liked it chunky not smooth. So it was different.

Chicken Salad

Roasting the chicken makes a better flavor for this chicken salad.

2 large chicken breasts

2 tablespoons olive oil

Salt and pepper to taste

½ cup halved green or red grapes

½ cup diced celery

½ cup roasted walnuts or pecans if you prefer

Mayonnaise to taste

1 tablespoon each fresh chopped oregano and thyme

1. Preheat the oven to 375 degrees.
2. In a small bowl, mix the olive oil, herbs and salt and pepper. Rub all over the chicken breasts.
3. Bake in a 375 degree oven for 35–40 minutes, checking for doneness. Remove from the oven and let cool.
4. After the chicken has cooled, pull it apart and chop it up. In a large bowl, mix in the grapes, celery and nuts.
5. Mix with enough mayonnaise to taste. Some people like a lot of mayonnaise some not so much. Make it to your taste.

Serve.

Often I'd make curried chicken salad. It was the same as above but I mixed 1 teaspoon curry powder into the mayo.

Inspired Blessings
Buddy's Jalapeno Pepper Jelly

Lucy Hairston is one of the most in-tune, generous and loving healer/psychic beings I've ever met. She is in touch with her "sources" via the dowsing tool she keeps in her pocket at all times, because you never know when you'll need some extra information. As we say, "She is so in touch with the spirit world and the psychic energy of healing she is barely tethered to earth." Our Dairy Barn attendees have learned to seek Lucy's help in many ways.

Lucy taught us what she learned from classes she took from Dr. Bradley Nelson. She explained how trapped emotions can create pain and disease in our bodies in this lifetime and from past lives. Lucy shared that trapped emotional energies can gather around the heart, creating a heart-wall that can block your body's energies. Releasing trapped emotions every day, as Lucy teaches, may result in the immediate departure of physical health problems and sometimes mental issues, as well.

She went through the five major processes that everyone can use and are all listed on Dr. Bradley Nelson's website. Every trapped emotion has an impact on your life. They affect us in many different ways, positively and negatively. She taught us how to discover those emotions and a process to release the pain that each emotion holds for us. She cautioned us about the side-effects of processing emotions and suggested ways to eliminate those effects. During questions and answers, someone asked her about how to dowse and she spent the rest of the day walking us through learning how to tune into the energies all around us.

Lucy's husband Buddy was a whiz at building things, gardening, composting, and making copper art. But, mostly for us, Buddy was a great cook. He shared this recipe for Hot Pepper Jelly which has become one of our favorite appetizers.

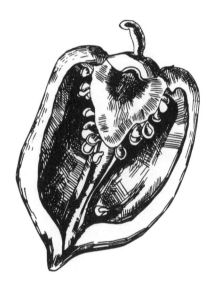

Hot Pepper Jelly

1 cup roughly chopped red bell peppers
$1/2$ cup roughly chopped jalapeno peppers
5 cups white sugar
$1^1/2$ cups apple cider vinegar
1 6 oz. container liquid pectin

1. Remove stems, veins and seeds from peppers, mince in food processor.
2. In a 5 quart pot over high heat combine everything BUT the pectin.
3. Bring to a boil and boil for 3 minutes.
4. Remove from heat and cool for 5 minutes.
5. Stirring constantly, add pectin mixture and cool for 2 more minutes. Then stir for one minute.
6. Pour into hot, sterilized jars and seal for canning.

Serve over a block of cream cheese and serve with crackers.

Follow Your Heart

Sweet Potatoes

In September of 2008, Carol Fitzpatrick made a presentation titled: *A Call to Remember: Follow Your Heart, Change the World*.

This is what she said: We have the power to radically change the course of humanity's future. We do it by changing ourselves. Carol then defined the process that can transform our lives, and everyone in our world. She taught us how to see the energy patterns in our lives and change them. Most of all, she reminded us that by taking the steps to transform our own lives, we are the change the world has been waiting for.

Carol Fitzpatrick is a modern-day mystic, author and healer who has been teaching and mentoring new paradigm leaders for over 25 years. Her message—"Follow your heart, change the world"—has evolved from a grassroots wake-up call into an international movement.

Carol's message is a staple for the soul.

Sweet potatoes are a staple of my diet. I love them and the first time I planted them, somehow I forgot what was growing in that particular bed. In the fall, when I was cleaning the beds for winter, I accidently dug up a sweet potato the size of a football. I was amazed and ended up with two five gallon buckets of sweet potatoes. I've never forgotten my sweet potatoes since.

Baked Sweet Potato

1 large sweet potato, washed, dried and wrapped in foil
1 tablespoon butter
1 tablespoon brown sugar
Pinch of cinnamon

1. Preheat the oven to 350 degrees.
2. Bake until you can squeeze the potato in the foil and it gives easily, approximately 45 minutes to an hour. Or you can stick a fork in it. If it goes through, it's done.
3. Add the butter, brown sugar and cinnamon.

Serve.

Creamed Sweet Potatoes

4–5 medium-size potatoes
1 can (8 oz) crushed pineapple
1 cup brown sugar
½ stick butter

1. Peel, cut up and boil four or five medium sized sweet potatoes until done. You can boil with the peeling on and it comes off easily after they cool a bit if you don't want to peel beforehand.
2. Pour off the water, add the pineapple, brown sugar, butter and mix well.

Serve

Holy Shifts

Apple, Walnut and Avocado Salad

In July of 2007 Karen Bloomberg and Dava Money came to speak to us about inviting holy shifts into our lives. They also presented exercises for learning to move through life consciously and with celebration. Karen was a Presbyterian minister with a side of shamanism thrown in; Dava is a psychotherapist.

The title of their talk was: "The Authenticity Series."

They started off explaining that we needed to honor our seeking to unite with the Divine, to know and appreciate God's spirit in each of us. In our hearts, they said, we are all mystics in these modern times. In the chaos of this world, we need to provide a sacred place to nurture our divine essence-that part of us that yearns for God.

They taught "action tools" to cultivate awareness of hidden issues that could be holding us back from our full potential. They gave us tools for intention setting and discovering our personal power. We were encouraged to write up a spiritual contract for ourselves and our relationships.

Karen A. Bloomberg Th.M. was a Presbyterian clergywoman, including 15 years as a pastoral counselor and workshop retreat facilitator. She specialized in integrating the essence of many faith traditions into practical and everyday living. Unfortunately, Karen has passed from this world to the next. We miss her sweet spirit.

Dava Money M.Ed. facilitates the integration of mind, body, and spirit as a means of evolving consciousness. Dava is a spiritual coach, author, trainer, and retreat facilitator and is also the founder of Creative Healing Institute and A School for Modern Mystics.

The talk was an enlightening experience for all of us, but…

As we were experiencing our inner mystic and enjoying Karen and Dava's talk, Karen suggested we go <u>outside</u> the Dairy Barn to the yard. There she would provide each of us a drum and suggested we make a shaman's circle.

Umm, I thought…this is a working farm and those farmers coming to get hay might get the wrong idea! There we'd be, thirty or more women, all ages, all sizes, beating on drums and chanting. This was something I was pretty darned sure the farmers I knew would have never, ever seen. I suggest we stay inside but it was difficult with the pews to make a full circle.

So we marched out; each of us were handed a drum as we passed out the door. There we were in the space between the Dairy Barn, the grain silos and the hay barn. Yes, we had plenty of room to spread out and create a circle. We started our chants and drumming.

Sure enough, we're in our mode, chanting and drumming, and here comes a very slow, very old, F-150 Ford pickup truck down the lane headed straight for us. A farmer here for some hay, I'm guessing. A local farmer with a farm-tan—darker from his eyes down from the constant sun, and a lighter, softer, pale white from his eyes up where his skin has been shaded by the cowboy hat he wears. He is staring out his window trying to make sense of it, trying to take it all in, a toothpick in his mouth, eyes glued on us, moving very slowly so he can get a good look. I'm sure my brother had arranged to meet him at the barn and put the round hay bale on his truck with the tractor and front-end loader but my brother was nowhere to be seen. Mr. Farmer slowly motored on around the circle driveway. We waved, we said hello. He gave a little tip of his hat.

Later my brother told me that when Mr. Farmer finally found him, he advised: "You better get over there to your hay barn because there are a bunch of women and they were acting weird. They might be witches."

My brother laughed and said, "They're looking for the Lord in their own special way."

God Bless my brother—an angel on earth if there ever was one!

Light hearts thrive on light, nourishing foods. We had so much lettuce and such a variety of lettuces that I made salads every day. The apples and the avocados were store bought but were delicious in the dressing.

Apple, Walnut and Avocado Salad

1 large head romaine lettuce, sliced or broken into pieces

2 firm apples chopped into bite-sized pieces

1/2 cups raisins

1/2 cups walnut pieces

1/2 cup broken sesame honey sticks

1/2 cup chopped celery

1 avocado, peeled, pitted and cut up

1/2 cup bleu cheese, crumbled

1/2 cup olive oil

1/4 cup balsamic vinegar

1 teaspoon Italian seasoning

3 tablespoons chopped fresh sweet basil

3 tablespoons chopped fresh parsley

Salt and pepper to taste

1. In a large bowl, mix lettuce, apples, raisins, walnuts, sesame honey sticks, celery, avocado and blue cheese.
2. In a container with a lid, mix the oil, vinegar, seasoning, basil and parsley. Put the lid on and shake vigorously to completely blend. Taste, add salt and pepper as needed.
3. Toss with salad.

Serve.

Note: Cooked sliced chicken is a perfect addition.

Edgar Cayce's Legacy
Corn and Cheese Chowder

A. Robert Smith, known to all as Bob, came to speak about his newest book in the spring of 2006, *No Soul Left Behind* as well as his older book *My Life as a Seer*. Bob was editor of *Venture Inward* in Virginia Beach and a great friend of Events at the Dairy Barn. He drove the 150 miles to attend many of our Events. I had been Bob's Literary Agent while I was in Manhattan and sold his book, *My Life as a Seer*.

As I've said, when my mother, Florence Martin, worked for one of the first Virginia Welcome Centers built in Virginia, she was required to visit all the tourist sights of Virginia. One of the places they traveled to was Edgar Cayce's A.R.E. Mom was impressed and purchased a book that she thought we'd enjoy, *There is a River* by Tom Sugrue. Every word in that book spoke to my soul. I loved Edgar Cayce's work and I have never stopped being impressed by his readings and his life. Mr. Cayce's work made a dynamic impression on both of us.

Bob's talk was about Edgar Cayce and his work. In it, he told us that in the annals of mysticism, few seers could match the lasting power and profound insight of Edgar Cayce. A clairvoyant philosopher of vast breadth and kindly demeanor, Cayce devoted his life to answering queries from tens of thousands seeking advice on their spiritual quests and personal affairs. His groundbreaking perceptions on the essence of healing, and on dreams, karma, and reincarnation served to inform and transform untold destinies.

Bob's talk was well received.

Bob is an award-winning journalist and the author of ten books, has been an editorial writer, and a former Washington correspondent covering Congress and seven presidents. He was also founding editor of A.R.E.'s member magazine, *Venture Inward* and its editor for 20 years

You may well be wondering how a news correspondent comes to write a life-changing book like *My Life as a Seer*. My guests at the Dairy Barn wondered, as well. He told us the story that day. It was so impressive I thought I'd include his blog. Bob explains how he was called to write the book that has had such a profound effect on its author and readers.

Finding the Lost Memoirs of Edgar Cayce

By A. Robert Smith

As a newspaper reporter for over 30 years, I had interviewed all kinds of people—from governors and presidents to scatterbrains and shysters—but no one like Hugh Lynn Cayce, the son of Edgar Cayce and then president of the A.R.E., who had invited me for lunch one day in 1980. Over white wine and crab salad, I agreed to write his biography.

Unknown to me at the time was that Hugh Lynn had previously asked Jess Stearn, the author of the bestselling book, *The Sleeping Prophet*; but Jess was too busy and had recommended me in his stead.

Hugh Lynn agreed to come to my house in Virginia Beach for long interviews every Sunday afternoon; and he told Gladys Davis Turner, who had been Edgar Cayce's secretary, to give me access to anything she had stowed in her bank-sized vault. That vault was so big that you could disappear inside of it while rummaging through Gladys' stacks of priceless documents. Nobody, I learned, had ever set foot in Gladys' treasure house without her permission.

In our interviews, Hugh Lynn gave me so many stories—about how his father saved him from blindness, his courtship of the prettiest girl in Virginia Beach, being in the Battle of the Bulge Army service under General Patton, and the ups and downs of creating the A.R.E.— that it took five years for me to complete the book. It was titled, *About My Father's Business*, but he died before he could read it. The process of writing it was great preparation for me in starting A.R.E.'s member magazine, *Venture Inward*, in 1984.

During the research process, I came across a marvelous find. Plowing around in Gladys' secret hideaway, I discovered a manuscript that looked like it had been dictated. I asked Gladys about it, and she said:

"Mr. Cayce started to tell the story of his life, and I just typed it up as he progressed."

"Did he finish it?" I asked.

"No. He was too busy giving readings."

Too bad he didn't complete it, I thought, but he was too focused on helping other people to tell his story.

Then I discovered another startling manuscript—a detailed narrative by Edgar's father, Leslie B. Cayce (aka, the "Squire"), about Edgar's childhood. Like a packrat, I made copies of both narratives and stowed them until I could figure out what to do with them.

I soon found a way to combine Edgar's life story with the Squire's account. Combining the two versions made for a more complete story.

The book was originally published by A.R.E. Press in 1997, and titled, *The Lost Memoirs of Edgar Cayce*. It was an instant bestseller among members and sold about 20,000 copies.

I liked Edgar's take on his life because he was so frank and honest about his feelings, even about when his first love, a girl named Bess, spurned him after her father told her that Edgar was a bit crazy. Sprinkled freely through his memoir are confessions of doubts, of uncertainty, of yearning to be "normal" rather than blessed with an astonishing talent. His admissions mark him as a truly humble man who never let adulation undermine his motive of service to others. He remained the living fulfillment of that saying of his, "If we ever get to heaven, it will be by leaning on the arm of someone we have helped."

Among those who read it was a literary agent, Sandra Martin. She told me she could sell it to a major New York publishing house, and did so with St. Martin's Press. They paid an enormous sum and published a hardback edition in 1997 under a different title, *My Life As a Seer*. Their hardback was sold internationally, at least in Japan and Canada, and was followed by a paperback edition. Those editions sold about 40,000 copies, and the paperback is still in print.

Now St. Martin's is publishing a digital edition (e-book) of *My Life as a Seer: The Lost Memoirs of Edgar Cayce* for readers who prefer an Amazon Kindle or the Barnes & Noble Nook.

So, sixty-nine years after Edgar Cayce's death, his fabulous story is still being circulated in the latest format—a story that will never die.

Corn on the cob was a summer staple and I've always loved corn chowder so I'd taken a package of corn I'd frozen and made soup. I made it especially for Bob because he loved it.

Corn and Cheese Chowder

4–5 ears corn, shucked and cleaned or 2 cups frozen

6–8 bacon strips, fried until crisp

1 medium onion, chopped

1 red pepper, chopped

¼ cup flour

3 cups chicken broth

2 cups half-and-half

1 cup grated cheese—cheddar or Swiss/whatever you like

1. Bring a large pot of water to boil. When boiling, drop the corn cobs carefully into the boiling water for 2 minutes. Remove. After they cool a bit, cut two cups of corn off the cobs. You can also use two cups of frozen corn.
2. In a large fry pan, cook 6 to 8 slices of bacon until crisp.
3. In a heavy pot, sauté the onion and red pepper until soft.
4. Add the crumbled bacon into the mixture.
5. After those have mixed and hot, add the corn until it is warmed through.
6. Then add the flour to cook for about 3 to 4 minutes.
7. Raise the temperature to high, and begin to add in the chicken stock and cream. Whisk constantly, cooking for 15 minutes.

Makes six servings. Serve with crusty French bread.

Psychic Kids
Pear and Romaine Salad

On September 20, 2008, we had Nancy Baumgarten come and talk to us about Psychic Kids. Nancy is the Director of Profound Awareness Alliance and the Enchanted Forest Intuitive Arts Camp for psychic children in Asheville, North Carolina.

As a mother Nancy noticed that her young daughter was different. She could see and hear people that Nancy couldn't see or hear. She came to the conclusion that her daughter was gifted with psychic abilities. She knew very little about psychic awareness and development but decided to educate herself with "discernment and balance." She shared her insights and discoveries.

Many of our attendees brought children and grandchildren to the meeting. Nancy offered hands-on experiential exercises to help understand the children's experiences as well as help the audience to realize their own gifts and abilities.

I've often wanted to open a restaurant that just served soups and salads because I make so many in so many variations. One of my all time favorite salads is the combined flavor of pears, parmesan, romaine and a tart and tasty vinaigrette. I made it for us that warm September day.

Pear and Romaine Salad

1 head romaine lettuce pulled apart

1 ripe pear cut up into bite-sized pieces

1/2 cup pieces walnuts

1/2 cup chopped celery

1/2 cup blue cheese

2 cups small bite-sized pieces dry bread

1 tablespoon Italian seasoning, divided

Oil for frying

1/2 cup olive oil

3 tablespoons pomegranate wine vinegar

Salt and pepper to taste

1. In a large bowl, mix the lettuce, pears, walnuts, celery and blue cheese.
2. Make the croutons by putting the bread in a large bowl. Toss with the Italian seasoning.
3. Heat the oil on high heat in a large fry pan. Add the bread and fry until crisp. Remove and dry on a paper towel.
4. Add to the top of the salad.
5. Make the dressing by putting the olive oil, vinegar and salt and pepper to taste in a jar or covered container and shake vigorously. Pour over all.
6. Toss.

Serve.

ESP
Pasta Alfredo Light

In May of 2011, Dr. Sally Rhine Feather, Director of the Rhine Research Center, came to speak to our group. When I called, she laughed and said she'd spoken in a lot of places but never in a Dairy Barn. I told her I'd heard that a few times. I assured her it was a sweet place.

This is the introduction she sent me describing her talk:

J.B. Rhine and his wife, Louisa Rhine, were responsible for the creation of the field of parapsychology. He adopted the term in order to give legitimacy to the field as a science. He brought the study of psychical research to the laboratory and set-up rigorous methods and concepts to further develop the understanding of what was considered, at the time, "uncommon human knowledge." Dr. Rhine originated the phrase ESP—extrasensory perception.

In her talk Sally shared with us how the psi of everyday life is most commonly expressed. She also reported on the latest Rhine parapsychology research on-going at the Rhine: Visualization Training and Real-life Goal Realization; Effects of Emotion and Attitude on Electronic Devices; The Experience of Healing;

Psychokinesis (PK): Existence, Limitations, and Mechanism; and Examining the Nature of Waking Intuition.

Our group had many questions about their own experiences. Sally graciously answered them all. It was a fascinating event.

Sally grew up in the world of parapsychology in Durham, North Carolina. She worked as a research assistant at the Duke Lab before and after a B.A. from the College of Wooster (1951) and as a researcher at FRNM after a doctorate in psychology (Duke University, 1967). Since 1995 she has been active at the RRC in various administrative roles, serving on two different occasions as volunteer Executive Director.

In 2005, she co-authored a book, *The Gift: ESP, the Extraordinary Experiences of Ordinary People* with Michael Schmicker. *The Gift* presented an update of Louisa E. Rhine's research and books on spontaneous ESP experiences.

Afterwards we had some pasta and salad because it was a little chilly in the Dairy Barn that day.

Pasta Alfredo–Light

1 box linguini, spaghetti or your favorite pasta

¼ cup ham (you can purchase sliced ham from the meat counter) cut into bite size pieces

½ cup feta cheese, crumbled

½ cup frozen baby green peas

½ stick of unsalted butter

½ cup of cream

1. Put a large pot of salted water over high heat to boil. Add the pasta and reduce the heat to simmer per the box's instructions.
2. After pasta cooks al dente, drain and put back in hot pot.
3. Stir in ham, cheese and green peas.
4. Cut the butter into chunks and drop in the pot.
5. Pour in the cream.
6. Lower the heat and slowly and gently toss the pasta until the cheese melts.
7. Add salt and pepper to taste.

Serves 4.

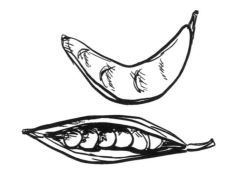

What It All Means

Ripe Tomatoes
from the Garden

Francis Sporer is a dear friend of the Dairy Barn. Retired now, he was artistic director of *Venture Inward*. An extraordinary artist, he moved from Missouri to Virginia Beach to learn more about Mr. Cayce's work.

In November of 2008, he gave us an overview based on Edgar Cayce's readings of how everything started, us/the earth/the universe, how we evolved and when we entered the play, how we got caught up here on the Earth and how we forgot who we are. Francis explained aspects of the mind, how the body/mind work together and how the unconscious keeps us from change even when change is beneficial.

The meaning of life according to the Edgar Cayce philosophy is that each person living on the earth is here for a specific soul purpose; a purpose that no one else can fulfill. While for some people, their purpose might be directly related to a profession or vocation, for others it could simply be a particular way of living day by day.

A morning filled with information, explanations and challenges to what we "think" we know.

We ended with a meditation.

Recipe #1: Tomatoes

Go to the garden and pick a plump, juicy, ripe tomato and eat it right there. Francis was concerned and cautioned us not to eat tomatoes that weren't totally ripe. Francis emphasized that point over and over. Okay, we got it.

Recipe #2: Tomatoes

Put sliced ripe tomatoes on toasted bread, spread mayonnaise, add lettuce, salt and pepper.

Recipe #3: Tomatoes

A slice of ripe tomato, a slice of fresh mozzarella, a basil leaf, and a little olive oil drizzled over and salt and pepper to taste.

Recipe #4: Tomatoes

Quarter four tomatoes and slice four cucumbers into 1 inch pieces, mix together with basil, mint a little minced garlic and a mix with olive oil, salt and pepper to taste.

Guided by Music

Spicy Sesame Noodles

In April of 2006, Carol Bush drove in from Virginia Beach to speak. Later, she moved to Bracey. Everybody loves Carol and she is a fantastic addition to our community.

Carol is a pioneer of a new therapy that uses classical music with guided imagery for profound changes of consciousness. She uses this special music while counseling her clients. She brought her music system to share with us so that we could experience the healing power of music first hand. The music, especially chosen for its evocative nature comes from the masterworks of classical tradition. It has been found that music listened to in a deeply relaxed state induces a dream-like flow of images and feelings that in turn inspire and stimulate creative problem solving and offer surprising insights.

Some of our Dairy Barn attendees had profound experiences; some of which they couldn't explain. One woman stopped coming because her experiences were so upsetting to her. It was an extraordinary day at the Dairy Barn.

Carol Bush is one of the pioneers of Guided Imagery and Music, known as GIM. Her thirty-five years of clinical experience have included a variety of mental health settings, and private practices in Miami, Florida and Virginia Beach and Bracey, Virginia. Her book, *Healing Imagery & Music: Pathways to the Inner Self*, which includes a special GIM music CD introduced this powerful new therapy to a mainstream audience. Carol has authored scholarly articles on the use of GIM for professional journals, and wrote a chapter on GIM for two books; *The Whole Mind* and *The Mozart Effect*. Carol has been a trainer of this method throughout the United States, as well as in Europe, Asia, South America and Mexico.

It was another chilly and rainy day at the Dairy Barn so I decided on something warm and spicy for lunch.

Spicy Peanut Sesame noodles

8 oz package regular spaghetti noodles, cooked per
   package instructions

1$\frac{1}{2}$ cups smooth peanut butter (any brand)

$\frac{1}{2}$ cup rice vinegar

$\frac{1}{4}$ cup soy sauce

2 tablespoons dark soy sauce

2 teaspoons minced garlic

2 to 6 chili or jalapenos peppers, mild to hot to taste

3 tablespoons sugar

$\frac{1}{2}$ teaspoon salt

$\frac{1}{2}$ cup toasted sesame oil

$\frac{1}{2}$ cup freshly brewed black tea

Cucumber strips, (optional)

1. In a bowl, mix the peanut butter, soy sauces, garlic, peppers,
   sugar and salt. Add the sesame oil and black tea and then
   pour over noodles.
2. Mix thoroughly, garnish with cucumber strips.

Serve.

Holistic Medicine
More Roasted Vegetables

L arry Burk, M.D., shared the story of his journey from mainstream medicine to alternative or holistic medicine. He filled us in on how many of the alternative medical practices work and taught us more about, EFT (Emotional Freedom Technique). It was August of 2008 and the Dairy Barn was very hot that day but Larry was such a great speaker that a some of the attendees came to me and quietly asked if he'd stay for the afternoon, after we had our lunch. They had many more questions they wanted to ask. That was a first. I asked Larry if he'd be open to it and he agreed. It was a spirited, emotional and powerful discussion for all of us. Larry was so inspired by his experience with us that he decided to write a book, *Let Magic Happen*.

He shared with us many insights he'd learned about healing with alternate methods. He said that many alternative medical practitioners believe that for true healing to occur, the root causes of disease need to be addressed. These causes may include toxins, dietary deficiencies, psychological traumas or spiritual issues. Often conventional medicine only treats the symptoms of a disease through suppressive therapies such as pharmaceuticals. A more useful approach, he said, is to look at symptoms as metaphors that are trying to draw our attention to a significant imbalance within the body-mind-spirit. Once the metaphor related to a symptom has been identified, approaches such as Emotional Freedom Techniques (EFT) can be used to address the underlying psychospiritual issues.

Often people unfamiliar with the holistic medical field assume that science—traditional western science—plays no role in the backgrounds of alternative practitioners. Larry's biography shows that this is not the case. Larry was formerly Director of Education at the Duke Center for Integrative Medicine, and he obtained a BA in Chemistry from Duke in 1977 and completed medical school and radiology training at the University of Pittsburgh. Following a year at the Pennsylvania Hospital, Dr. Burk spent four years as Assistant Professor at Thomas Jefferson University Hospital in Charlottesville. In 1993 Dr. Burk returned to Duke University as an Associate Professor of Radiology and co-founded the Duke University Medical Center's Mind-Body Medicine Study Group. Dr. Burk has made presentations on research methodology in intuitive diagnosis at the NIH Conference on CAM Research Methodology and the Parapsychological Association. Dr. Burk left Duke in 2004 to start his own consulting company, Healing Imager, Inc. specializing in musculoskeletal teleradiology and Emotional Freedom Techniques.

If you are interested in deepening your knowledge on holistic healing methods, you might visit Larry's website, *Let Magic Happen*.

If you are searching for a recipe based on whole, natural foods, to begin the healing process, you might try one of these.

Recipe #1: Roasted Vegetables

Zucchini, red and yellow peppers, and onions,
    cut into 2 inch pieces
¼ cup olive oil
Parsley, Basil and Rosemary sprigs to taste
Salt and pepper to taste

1. Preheat the oven to 400 degrees.
2. In a very large bowl, mix the vegetables with the oil and herbs.
3. Taste and adjust the salt and pepper.
4. Spread the vegetables across a cookie sheet and cook at 400 degrees until tender, about 15 minutes.

Serve

Recipe #2: Roasted Vegetables

4–5 medium sized white potatoes
2 cups 2–3 inch diced carrots
2 cups 2–3 inch diced peeled sweet potatoes
2 cloves garlic, sliced
1 large onion, quartered
Herbal sprigs: rosemary, thyme and/or parsley
1/2 cup olive oil

1. Preheat the oven to 400 degrees.
2. Put the potatoes, carrots and sweet potatoes into a large bowl.
3. Add salt and pepper to taste.
4. Add the herbs and mix in enough olive oil to moisten all.
5. Spread the vegetables on a sheet pan and roast for 35–45 minutes.

These vegetables go well with beef or pork roasts. It is sturdy and good for winter meals as well.
Serve.

The Dairy Barn was a magnificent place to bond with new and old friends. There is nothing better than to participate in the joy of like-minded people, speaking your truth. The men and women who spoke shared their hard-earned life wisdom from their hearts to our receptive hearts and minds. The teachings by friends and speakers inspired, motivated and moved us forward to the next level. To the understanding that we are all one family, one spiritual, universal, united humanity. Each of us is on "the path" whatever we believe that path to be and, of course, it is up to us how we walk that spiritual journey.

I have a grateful heart for each of the speakers who took the time and made the effort to drive to Bracey to share their message, their knowledge and their wisdom with us. I realize now that their messages were far reaching. Much farther than any of us could imagine at the time.

On Being Famous
Caponata Appetizer

My business trip to Los Angeles had been nothing but back to back television pitch meetings and prickly personalities. We were finally landing at Dulles Airport, outside of Washington, D.C., for a change of planes. Thank goodness. As a literary agent in New York City, trips to LA were a necessary part of the business. But it was always good to be going home. Dulles has trams that take you from the plane to the terminal for your baggage. The plane was full so we were all milling around on the tarmac and then piling in to the next empty tram that drove up. As I was last on the last tram, I sat in the only available space and we chugged off. I pushed back in my seat with my suitcase between my legs and looked around. Everyone was looking at me, that entire tram was full of people just looking at me.

Ah, I said to myself, I've had this experience before. I turned to my seatmate, bent my head in confidence and said conspiratorially, "I had this happen to me once before when I worked at the University of Georgia." My seatmate turned and totally focused her attention on me. So I continued. "I was taking the bus across campus. The seats were against the sides of the bus in front and parallel in back. I sat in front and glanced to the back of the bus and it seemed that everyone was looking at me. I looked down to make sure my blouse was buttoned. I looked all around me and nothing seemed amiss. But they kept staring. A friend got on the next stop and sat across from me and we talked a bit. Still, when I glanced towards the back of the bus everyone had their eyes glued on me. It was spooky."

My friend and I got off at the Ecology building and I asked her if she noticed that everyone was staring at me. First she looked blankly at me and then laughed out loud, "Sandra, you were sitting next to the most famous guy in Georgia: Herschel Walker, running back for the University of Georgia football team. They were looking at him, not you."

I told that story to this beautiful woman sitting next to me who everyone was actually looking at, not me, and who was paying cautious attention to me. Her studious and serious face broke into a smile and she laughed at the story. It was the actress Glenn Close; star of *Fatal Attraction* and at that time, the TBS series *Damages*.

There's something about that story.

Lately I've observed that friends have felt that everyone was looking at them, but symbolically. They see themselves reflected back in everyone's eyes. One had made a call to ask someone to do her a favor and then couldn't understand why she didn't stop everything, hop right on it and get it done. She thought the world revolved around her and whatever she thought was important superseded everything else. "Couldn't she see how important this was?" she kept asking me. She could only see the world through her eyes.

Another woman, a business friend, was focused on a group of Manhattan businessmen, potential investors, who'd called to ask her opinion on a different business venture they were considering. She had had experience in that type of venture. She was certain they were anxiously awaiting her expert advice and spent the following days dithering on and on about the exact right thing to say. When she finally returned their call, they asked what her call was about. They didn't recall that they'd reached out to her.

It is funny how we operate in our own self-constructed little worlds and how our minds can build on the nearest nothing to make something big of it or, conversely, take a big event and ignore it.

The "me" generation is creating a culture that operates not on the Golden Rule—"do unto others as you would have them do unto you"—but the Wall Street Rule: "Take care of me first, no matter the cost to others." From Facebook to human potential groups, whatever it is, it is all about me. Not only does this "me-ism" separate us as a human family, it creates a condition where it's every person for themselves, not trusting anyone's motives.

How did this all come about?

Betty Friedan's book, *The Feminine Mystique* was published in 1963 and Gloria Steinem launched *Ms. Magazine* in 1969. By then I had two growing children. During the mid-70s, the women's consciousness raising movement was in full swing, but I didn't feel it was talking about my life or to me. I read the articles in magazines about the women's movement. I read the negative opinion pieces in the local newspaper about how it was going to ruin the family. But in the 70s I was living a life of someone else's design and expectations. My being was shaped by who I was expected to be—by parents, husband, and my southern environment. I never gave a thought about what I wanted in any deep way. Thoughts about my self-esteem never occurred to me. Those feminist consciousness-raising groups were for other women, not me.

Instead I met a spiritual teacher; George Ritchie, a consciousness raiser like no one else. Dr. Ritchie always made a point of asking the women attending his lectures or meetings or even social gatherings what their opinion was, and if they had suggestions, and what did they think about the subject. He listened and took their responses seriously.

One of his lectures was on Individuality and the Evolving of

Consciousness. In it he told us that originally people were united by clans, tribes; one leader served the good of all and, if he didn't he was thrown out or killed. Then countries and dictators made decisions that served all for good or bad. Men were consistently the power forces. Rarely were women able to command. And when they were it wasn't much different.

Dr. Ritchie said that he believed that eventually every single person was going to have to figure out who they were, what they believed, and act on their own inner knowledge; men, women and even children. Especially, he said, it was women's values we needed. As women, we had to "come into our own," to learn who we were and, as women, we had to form our own opinions, our own values and to discover what we stood for in the world.

I certainly walked that path and as I discovered my inner strengths and formed my own opinions, I encouraged my kids to do the same, especially my daughter.

Today it seems we've made that individuality leap.

As a literary agent and television producer in New York City on subjects like consciousness, spirituality and new science, I was open to the next evolutionary moment. Some of my first clients, unknown to all but a few, became household names. It was an amazing journey.

I'd met the world famous medical intuitive and award winning author, TV star and lecturer, Caroline Myss. We became great friends. She is straightforward, smart and savvy. I like those qualities in my friends.

We happened to both be in Los Angeles one spring. She was giving a lecture and staying at the Hotel Bel Air. I was in LA for meetings with producers, studios and staying with old friends.

On another lovely day, as every day is lovely in LA, I drove to Beverly Hills to have lunch at the Bel Air with Caroline. After hellos, air kisses, ordering and eating, we were totally into it. We were having an intense, in depth, convoluted, multi-dimensional conversation. We were sitting by a big window looking out on a small pond with the Bel Air's famous white swans floating peacefully by like beauty queens. A great contrast to our powerful energy vortex.

The hostess, a pretty young girl, kept walking by. Each time she did she asked if we needed anything, "No thanks, we were fine," and she'd stand there for an extra second or so, and then leave. After the third or fourth time Caroline said, "She must recognize me from my television special. It has been airing on PBS. This happens to me all the time."

Then we dived back into our conversation about mysticism, time travel and the State of the World organization, who was doing what to whom. Our hostess cruised by again.

Caroline looked up at her and said, "What is it?"

That young lady stopped, looked right at *me*, and said, "Do you live in Virginia Beach? I'm pretty sure I recognize you." Yes, I did live in Virginia Beach, a long time ago, but now I live in Manhattan."

She remembered me from the first television series I ever did on a Norfolk, Virginia television station. It was a weekly interview show where I interviewed experts on meditation, dreams, the psychic Edger Cayce and Native American spirituality experts.

As she walked away, Caroline laughed and laughed, "Well, that'll show me."

Years passed. Life moved on. I retired from the literary agent business and moved back to the farm I grew up on in Southside Virginia. A film crew flew in to interview me for a documentary they were producing on a former literary client of mine. The director in his beret was quirky and very LA, although he said he'd flown from his home in Las Vegas. The executive producer was quiet and charming. I was well and truly nervous about the interview. I was used to being on the other side of the camera. The interview took most of the afternoon in my living room and then a little walking and talking filmed in my flower garden and finally it was done.

After such an anxious day, in nervousness, my heightened state of awareness, I asked the guys if they wanted to go to the local winery, Rosemont, and have a glass of wine. They were definitely up for that. The quirky director knew a great deal about growing grapes for wines so I introduced him to Stephen, the owner of the winery. He asked lots of questions. Then they moved to the bar for a wine tasting. I got a glass of my favorite wine and tried to gather myself and calm my worrying and questioning self about every word I'd uttered in the interview. After a bit, they rejoined us and we moved to a bigger table.

As we discussed the day, I noticed that a woman my age at a nearby table kept looking at us. I asked Stephen who she was, commenting to the guys: "She is probably somebody I went to school with and now that I'm back all these people I grew up with come up to me and I have no idea who they are." Stephen said he didn't know her, but he'd check it out and went to sit at their table. Lots of pointing and talking and looking our way ensued.

Finally, Stephen came back and said, "They think they recognize your friend here from a PBS series he has been hosting." We turn and looked at Robert, in his jaunty beret. He was smiling from ear to ear. Yes sir, it was him, Robert M. Knight, the famous photographer, not me, they were gawking at. Within a few minutes, Robert had a line of admirers asking for autographs. They'd watched his award-winning feature length documentary *Rock Prophecies*. They wanted autographs *and* to ask questions about one rock star or another they'd seen on the special which had recently aired on PBS.

His friend, the executive producer of their film, and I just moved away from the table and watched. He said, "This always happens to him." We tried to blend in to the background. We drank our wine and enjoyed the show.

Fame, it's a quirky thing.

This recipe was given to me by JoAnn Courter. JoAnn and her husband Buck were hard workers making the Dairy Barn presentable for events. She made it for some of our Dairy Barn Events and parties and everyone loved it. Including me.

Caponata Appetizer

3 med. eggplants (peel if you prefer, but not necessary)

1$\frac{1}{2}$ cups olive oil

4 onions, thinly sliced

$\frac{1}{2}$ cup tomato sauce

4 stalks celery, thinly sliced

$\frac{1}{2}$ cup drained capers

12 green olives, pitted and cut

1 tablespoon pine nuts

$\frac{1}{2}$ cup wine vinegar (you can use good balsamic and omit the sugar)

$\frac{1}{4}$ cup sugar

$\frac{3}{4}$ teaspoon salt

$\frac{1}{2}$ teaspoon pepper (add crushed red pepper if you want it a little spicy)

If you want it a little richer you can add tomato paste

1. Cut up eggplant and sauté in a little olive oil.
2. Add remaining oil and onions and brown.
3. Add tomato sauce and celery and cook until celery is tender (adding a little water if necessary).
4. Add capers, olives, pine nuts.
5. Heat vinegar in a small saucepan, dissolve sugar in vinegar and pour over eggplant.
6. Add salt and pepper and simmer 20 minute stirring frequently.
7. Cool before serving.
8. This will keep well a long time in the refrigerator--place in glass jars.

Serve as a side dish or sandwich filling or antipasto dip.

Speaking of Being Famous
Navy Bean Soup

When I had an office at ICON Productions at Warner Brothers in Los Angeles, I met many people in the movie making business. One of those was Carolyn MacDonald. She was head of Danny Glover's production company and a creative, savvy businesswoman if I ever met one. She was a beautiful woman with multiple talents—producing, writing and scrambling for money.

She was also from the South. We bonded over apple pie after an already long lunch talking about North Carolina where she was from—"Girl you never saw so much tobacco!" and Virginia where I was from—"I worked in those tobacco fields every summer of my life; the watermelon was the best though," and, naturally, how grateful we were to be away from the country and in the big city where we belonged. We always managed to get together when I was on the West Coast.

As is often the case when you're working in this arena you rarely met the "stars" because they are often out making movies in some distant land or on an extended vacation or just taking a break from working. They rarely hung around the office.

After a year or so of nudging some of my authors' books on Carolyn, she suggested I meet with Danny to pitch him one I'd recently sold. We were to meet at the Bel Air Hotel in Beverly Hills.

Now, as I've said, the Bel Air is a place apart. It is located in a residential area, up in the hills, and if you don't know where you're going, it is a hard place to find. Tranquil, lush, and hidden away. I never did see where people actually stayed because there were so many distractions with ornate gardens and lily ponds with speckled royal white swans.

Our brunch was on Sunday and Danny had been scheduled for a morning walk for a cancer cure. Carolyn was driving north from way down south of LA and, since I lived nearest, I got there first. We had reservations.

I'd had lunch, dinner and breakfast at the Bel Air before but this was the first time I was shown to one of the banquettes against the wall, two little steps up from the "common" area. Gorgeous, plush, red leather booths. I ordered coffee and looked at all the other diners looking at me, wondering who the heck I was. I am certain they were as perplexed as I was about how I was in this sacred space.

Finally, Danny arrived. He is a big guy, smiling, happy and very friendly. He had in his hand a little case that looks like a kid's lunch box. When I ask him what's in it, he says, "I like to keep my herbs and ayurvedic remedies with me."

Goodness. I liked that, indeed.

Carolyn arrived and we were chatting away about life and LA, and about cancer and the way medicinal herbs would be of such service to cancer sufferers.

People are coming and going and I am not paying attention. But I see that Danny is. He is seated directly across from me; Carolyn is in the middle between us. I notice that Danny seems to be paying more attention to the booth behind us than to us.

Finally, he says, "Sandra, scoot over I'm going to move over and sit next to you. Is that okay?"

"Sure."

Carolyn slides around and Danny changes seats.

He leans in close: "Have you noticed who is sitting directly behind us?"

"No."

"Steven Spielberg, George Lucas, the head of Universal Studios and the most powerful agent in LA. Those four guys must be worth 40 billion dollars, don't you think?"

He leans back a bit, cocking his head to one side, sizing me up. "You look like you're a strong country girl, and I think, between you and me, I think we could take them, don't you, girl?"

I was so surprised that I burst out laughing and the three of us laughed loud and long.

Danny is an accomplished actor, a great spirit with a good heart and boisterous sense of humor. He is also a very humble man.

Navy Bean Soup seemed like a perfect complement to this story. Beans are full of air and make you puff up, like some LA folk. I love the soup and buy local navy beans to make my soup. When I don't have local beans I use canned beans, which are just as good.

Navy Bean Soup

1 15 oz can of Navy or Great Northern Beans

3 strips bacon, diced

1 carrot, thinly sliced

1 small onion, thinly sliced

1 jalapeno, seeds removed and thinly sliced

1. Put the bacon in a two-quart pot and fry it until almost crisp.
2. When the bacon is about half way done, put in the carrots, onion and jalapeno.
3. Cook for about 5 minutes more.
4. Add the Navy Beans or Great Northern Beans and ½ can of additional water.
5. Cook, simmering for 15 minutes.

Serve.

Events at the Dairy Barn, Moving Along
Desserts

Dairy Barn Events were perking along. I was working in my garden, cooking and freezing vegetables and entertaining friends from my old life and meeting new friends on Lake Gaston. I was decompressing from the stress of Manhattan and life seemed pretty good. All my life I've tried to present a positive attitude and not complain. I always felt that unless a problem was something I could rectify, get rid of or change, I should just be quiet and live with it.

New York was anxiety producing, in the extreme, stressful every day, every hour almost. Just going out on the street was a little unsettling for those of us not brought up in a noisy, in-your-face environment. My flight or fight response was always on, just in case. For my clients, I tried to present an official, "Don't worry, I can take care of everything" attitude, but mostly I was the duck gracefully floating across the pond while underneath, I was paddling like hell.

I worked from my apartment on the Upper Westside. I was told, and found it true, that it was the only way I could make a profit as a literary agent—low overhead was the key. When I made the deal with Discovery I was told I had to open a "real" office.

I found a good deal, for NYC, at 52nd and Broadway. Originally, I'd applied for an office space in the building across the street, 53rd and Broadway, the Ed Sullivan Theater. Things were moving along nicely when my real estate agent called and said that the owner, CBS, had withdrawn the space. It was no longer available for rent. A few months later a big sign went up: *David Letterman Coming to the Sullivan Theater*. Well, that explains that.

I was unsure about everything. I had no mentor, other than the book, *How To Be Your Own Literary Agent*; and, at first, was not exactly welcomed into the tight knit group of editors and agents in Manhattan. I can't tell you how many times I was told: "You're really smart for a southerner." Like it was supposed to be a compliment. Son of a gun.

That kind of prejudice wasn't even my biggest problem. My biggest problem was that I'd been raised to be a people pleaser. The oldest of four, I'd spent a lifetime taking care of people, making sure everyone was comfortable, had what they needed, and after all that was taken care of, then me.

Often that left little time for me, so much so that when I finally came to myself, I didn't even know what "I" wanted. I'd been in so many self-encounter groups that I'd lost count. I'd been re-birthed, re-programmed, explored my childhood, re-evaluated my first marriage, my second marriage, my past lives, had life-changing psychic readings and spent hours in therapy.

It seemed to me that every author or want-to-be author and researcher in the mind-body-spirit genre wanted to have me represent him or her and, unfortunately, I couldn't represent everyone. Even so, years before Google, I would help writers to get their proposals together. We'd go over outlines and chapters over long, long phone calls. I'd suggest co-authors or ghost writers. This took up huge amounts of my time. I found that over the long run, it was a thankless job. Rarely did anyone think they needed help. Everyone had told them they should write a book. Other agents were jumping on the "new age and self help" bandwagon and I passed their names along.

Every psychic who pitched a book gave me a reading, whether I wanted one or not. I'd try to discourage them by sharing research that parapsychologists had observed: when psychics had an emotional energy, positive or negative, invested in a psychic reading, it was rarely a good reading. I never lied or fudged. I said, as clear as I could, when they were correct and when they were incorrect.

Even potential clients who weren't astrologers, but valued the advice of astrologers, wanted to see my astrology chart before sharing their story. Then, of course, every professional astrologer had to request my birth data so that they could read my chart before meeting with me. Since I had the Sun and Jupiter in the Ninth House of Publishing that made it okay for them to pursue me, but more often, I was not interested. After a few years of this, I kept copies of my astrology chart, Eastern and Western versions, in a nearby convenient file.

Psychic mediums told me about loved ones who were standing around me insisting I take them on as a client. Some psychics, year after year, made multiple attempts to get my attention. My dead grandmother, or grandfather, or aunt or uncle, figured prominently in these scenarios.

Every New Age or consciousness author or want-to-be author and researcher wanted to have me represent him or her, it seemed to me. I know that wasn't true but I had such a self-imposed burden that it was my job to bring this "world" to the mainstream public that I took on far too many clients and clients that hadn't developed their "story;" they just weren't ready. And then there was the ability to write. Many in the field were extreme right brain people and linear writing was a difficult task for them. Often, they had a great story, a great process to share, but couldn't get the story down on paper. It was difficult for them to write cogently, staying on track, or building to a conclusion.

Still, running a company in NYC, making money to pay employees, cover the rent (oh my God) utilities, taxes and entertaining clients was a daily trial.

Trying to do everything all the time was pretty darned hard. Even for me. I always had huge amounts of energy and made decisions quickly. Yes, I was a fast learner and savvy negotiator even if I was southern. I wasn't really prepared for this career but I had it none the less. I used to say, I made every mistake known to man and then some. That phrase learning on the job described me to a tee. Thankfully, there were several editors who decided to be "my friend" and they gave me good advice. One editor I house-sat for after my first sublet was up. She was away helping Ram Dass write his book. She was a godsend and a good-hearted soul, if ever there was one.

It was just that I was so passionate about what I was selling. I believed in New Age, Self-Help and Spiritual Books! And I was convinced that these manuscripts, these new authors were paradigm changers; that they had new takes on old wisdom that we, as a collective, needed to see, to hear, needed to process and convert to new ways of living to change ourselves and to change the world. I talked to every editor who'd see me and eventually I started selling manuscripts.

I learned about contracts and I loved every single one I received. Publishing houses spread the contract payments out as long as possible, but my bills were regular as clockwork and many, many times I couldn't pay my office rent while waiting on a publishing house to send a check.

Once, I remember confirming an appointment with an editor as I was to hand-deliver a manuscript that morning and we (the agency on behalf of the client) had not received the "check on signing" or the "check on delivery." I told the editor I wouldn't deliver the manuscript until I had a check. I'll never forget what the editor whined: "But the checks are written in New Jersey." I told him that as far as I knew there was transportation between New Jersey and New York City and until he had the check in his hand, I was keeping the manuscript in my hand.

He called back later, and quietly said, "I have your check."

My, my, wasn't that simple. I was learning.

I was just getting publishing down, understanding the rules and finding out who made decisions and who didn't, when I got *the* call about my proposal for the dream series. I'd officially submitted my proposal to The Discovery Channel (this was back when they only had the one channel, now they have fourteen or maybe more) three times and had been rejected three times. Still, I felt strongly that Discovery was the "one." In January of 1992 I got a call from the executives at Discovery; "We're in Manhattan today, do you want to have dinner tonight?"

They had decided to produce my television series on Dreams. I'd spent years working at a small PBS network in Norfolk, Virginia. What I didn't know about big time production was a huge amount. I'd had my own little local TV interview show and I had many friends in the TV business. That didn't really mean a thing.

I'd suggested a production crew that I knew and knew they knew the field so I felt comfortable with them. Discovery, not so much. They said no. I spent, with Discovery's help, months looking for the right fit. Afterwards, I realized that there was only one fit and that I wasn't reading Discovery's signs for a senior producer. Discovery's producer and I really didn't see eye to eye on the subject of dreams but she was very much in the eye of the Executive Producer from Discovery. These were the times I wish I'd had someone older, wiser and savvier to say, "Sandra, what they are trying to say is 'this is who we will be using' and so just say yes." Only when the films were completed did I realize that that woman was great at what she did. I had the concept but I only knew the content, the meaning, and the power of dreams; she knew how to make them visible. I will be forever grateful to her.

By that time, Big Name Publishers (people I'd only read about in the trades) were asking to meet with me for dinner, in a quiet, out-of-the-way restaurant so they could quiz me on what I thought the "next big trend" was going to be. I'd been lucky, so far. All the book trends I'd "sold" the publishers were successful. Wildly successful, which did not surprise me, but New York publishers were totally flummoxed by it.

In these dinner meetings, they'd nod their heads towards the Hudson River and ask, "What's happening out there?" Because they weren't "on the path" the entire burgeoning field was mystery to them.

It was during this time that I learned about people who were change agents, game changers; people who come in and upset the applecart. Publishers were telling me that after my full-court press to every editor who'd stand still long enough for me to tell them about the changes in consciousness, what these 50 million people I kept telling them about wanted to read, and that they'd better start publishing in my genre if they wanted to make money. Many publishers had gone "all in," started New Age imprints, hired editors, pumped up their marketing departments to accommodate the growing field. One publisher I lunched with profusely thanked me and told me these books had saved her publishing imprint from being shut down. It was a consciousness movement whose time had come even if the people making the money didn't understand how it was happening.

I remember having a conversation with an editor of mass market paperback books. He was truly perplexed. He'd published one of my authors and this was the author's third or fourth book and the editor, with a puzzled expression leaned in and said, "I want to ask you a question. Who are these 200,000 people? They'll buy this guy's next book within weeks of it coming out? How do they know? Why is it just that number—is it a cult or something? Each book sells a little over 200,000 and no more. But who are the buyers? We have no idea."

Of course, I knew who they were. I saw them at every conference I attended. I listened to them on the phone day after day. They wanted to change the world. They wanted to open the windows and doors to let all the secrets out.

Secrets: Once while waiting for an elevator I observed a man with a heavier coat than necessary for the weather speaking into his sleeve. I watched him as he watched the door of the building. A well-dressed man with a briefcase came in, with very serious demeanor, and a worried expression on his face. He pushed for the elevator and then stood quietly. The sleeve-talker whispered something as he stood behind the briefcase guy. They got on the elevator together going up to the Bantam-Doubleday-Dell floor. I decided to wait and see who came down. I am often early for appointments, so I had time. I took out a manuscript and started reading it. The sleeve-talker was back down in five minutes. I waited. I fussed with my manuscript bag. He just leaned against the wall looking out on Fifth Avenue. No more sleeve-talking. After 10 or 15 minutes, the briefcase guy walked out of the elevator. He looked determined, head down, he headed out the door. He didn't have his briefcase. The sleeve-talker talked into his sleeve again and followed the now, briefcase-less guy. He turned left and walked uptown. I thought I'd see where this was going, so I followed along, too. After a block, the sleeve-talker made an almost imperceptible nod of his head to a man standing across the street, dressed in a business suit. He nodded back. The sleeve-talker got in one of Manhattan's ubiquitous black town cars. The other fellow crossed the street and there we were; three in a line, all on one block. The briefcase-less guy, the business-looking guy and me; I'd been invisible to all three, but I was following along. We'd started at 53rd Street and after a few streets the briefcase-less man took a left and hurried into a parking garage. The business-looking guy followed him. I decided that I needed to get back to my appointment.

By now I was late for that appointment but as soon as I walked into the office of the editor, I described the scene, the man and asked if he'd been in their section. As calm as I'd been during the previous 30 minutes now I was super excited. The editor hadn't seen anything and we talked about my newest client and manuscript. But I didn't forget about it.

Months later, I was telling this story at a party, while I was in Washington, D.C. meeting potential authors and others. During that visit I'd been told by a high-ranking politician that "he was kept abreast of my movements"—whatever that meant, I had no idea. Looking back on my life so many times I was so foolish. I was a woman on a mission and I had no idea that this was dangerous ground.

Someone I trusted, at the time, had told me that I should be careful. He said there were those who didn't want the "unwashed" (his words) public getting the idea that they could psychically access information about anything, anywhere and during any time period. Still, I had no idea. Why would anybody want to stop that kind of empowering information was beyond me. I was successfully selling books in the genre and by now I'd also moved on to television. I met with every television and cable programmer who'd see me to pitch my authors and their books. I shared my ideas and my understanding that we were in the midst of a huge change in consciousness, hence the books on self-help, psychics and mediums and near death, as well as the lesser selling but still building world of UFO, conspiracy and ancient mysteries books. Television executives were paying attention to what was happening, too.

Later that year, the same high ranking politician's office "person" asked if I wanted to "join" their team. I'd be reporting on who was doing what and with whom. Keeping them in the loop with who the new psychics were and any new information I heard. Nothing hard for me, he'd said, you're so deep in the field it'd be easy money. The truth was I was already spreading that information around everywhere. I said, no, that is not for me and I cut ties with that organization. But I don't think they cut ties with me.

I was overwhelmed with new concepts about self-help, deep mysticism, and new pathways to wisdom. I was attending as many conferences as I could. I was also now a consultant or on the boards of spiritual organizations and parapsychology foundations. After I managed to get through the production of the Dream series (I think I sold 12 or 13 books on dream interpretation during those years) then the next trend: ancient mysteries; UFOs; and conspiracy manuscripts started to cross my desk. I was working 18 hour days, seven days a week for many years.

After 9/11 I took a break and then decided to quit being an agent. I was really burned out. I went to work for a new television network based in West Virginia. That didn't last long as the owner passed away and the network was sold. So, in late 2004, I moved back to the farm in Bracey. I bought a house on the Lake and planted my garden. We started having speakers at the Dairy Barn. I was happy. I had money. I had the best credit rating you can have. Life was good.

It was a nice October afternoon in 2007 when Joe, a friend I'd worked with in West Virginia, called to say that he'd retired and purchased a house in Virginia Beach and didn't I say that I'd moved to Virginia? Where exactly? Was I close to Virginia Beach? Nope, two plus hours away, but we reconnected. He lived on the oceanfront and so I visited him more than he visited me. It was wonderful talking about the spiritual, metaphysical and the self-help world. Talking about how we could've made great TV if only. We bemoaned the fact that our benefactor had died and the network had been sold.

Joe had spent his entire career in the television and cable business. He was knowledgeable about all facets of television and all the complexities of the country's cable systems. He had a comprehensive marketing and media background. Also, Joe was a deeply spiritual man. He should've been a minister. He had a wise and astute wife. I liked her a lot.

He and his wife attended a party Lake friends had for me for my 60th birthday. That weekend we talked and I could see that he was getting bored with Virginia Beach. He was used to the crazy, wild world of television, traveling to one city after another, conference calls, meetings and endless negotiations. I, of course, didn't miss that at all, but I did miss the promise of a television network focused on consciousness, spirituality, alternative health, and ancient mysteries. I knew what we could have produced would've meant a great deal to the potential audience of 50 million people pollster and researcher Paul Ray deemed "Cultural Creatives."

One October morning, a year later, I got a call from my Virginia Beach friend. Joe told me he couldn't take retirement any longer and he'd gone to work for Verizon in New York City. They were starting a new television network, FIOS and they'd asked him to join their team.

"Congratulations," I said, "that's great. Did you sell your house in Virginia Beach? I really liked visiting you there."

"No, I'm keeping the house. This is television and it might be a short-lived experiment. But, Sandra, it is a great opportunity for you. I'm calling to tell you that I can give you a television network of your own to produce the kind of programming that you and I think is important. FIOS-TV is just starting out and it is small and has no "subs" (for subscribers) yet, but it will."

I was speechless. Before my mind could react tears were streaming down my cheeks. This was my dream come true. I had no idea that this could happen.

That was the end of my peaceful easy life. The next few years were a time of crazy busy; focused fundraising, strategic TV proposals, savvy investors, potential money making deals, documenting the potential audience, and then re-writing a hundred times investor proposals, travel all over the US, meetings-endless meetings, conference calls ad nauseam, investors big and small, potential hosts, potential themes, potential subject matter, reality show pitches, documentary development, long-form series, short-form series, potential writers, endless meetings with tech people telling us what we needed, hiring management, and on and on. This went on for five years and I put all I had into it.

I lost everything. All my money, my house, my health and I think I lost my mind every now and then.

Life is about dealing with whatever happens. Doing what I can when I can and meanwhile maintaining my spiritual practices.

Favorite Dairy Barn Desserts

Date and Pear Cake

Serves 10

You'll need a 9-inch baking pan, make sure you butter and flour it so the cake does not stick.

1 cup pitted dates
1 cup water
1 teaspoon baking soda
1¼ cups all-purpose flour
¼ teaspoon salt
¼ teaspoon baking power
½ cup butter, softened
1¼ cups sugar
1 egg
1 teaspoon vanilla
½ cup shredded coconut
Powdered sugar for decoration
1 pear peeled and chopped
½ cup water
½ cup sugar

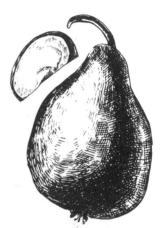

1. Preheat oven to 350 degrees.
2. In a small saucepan bring water to a boil. Drop in the dates. When the mixture is boiling, stir in baking soda (mixture will foam) and set it aside to cool.
3. In a large bowl, mix the dry ingredients: flour, salt and baking powder and set aside.
4. In another large bowl, beat butter, sugar, egg and vanilla until

combined.

5. Slowly add in the cooled date mixture to the butter and egg mixture until combined. Add the flour mixture gradually, beating until just combined. Fold in the pear and coconut.

6. Spread evenly into prepared 9-inch spring form baking pan or heart shaped cake pan.

7. Bake 45 to 50 minutes at 350 degrees or until toothpick comes out clean.

8. Cool and then carefully remove from pan. Sprinkle with powdered sugar.

9. Slice a pear carefully. Combined ½ cup of water and ½ cup of sugar and bring to a boil, stirring all the while. Add the pear slices. Cook gently for 10 more minutes until tender.

10. Allow to cool and then with a slotted spoon, top the cake with pears.

11. Arrange the pears and add more powdered sugar.

Serve.

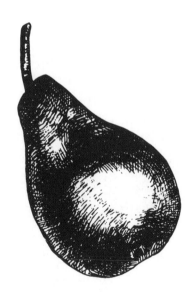

Magic Bars

Magic Bars are scrumptious. The recipe is on the back of the Eagle Brand Sweetened Condensed Milk.

Preparation time: 30 minutes

1^1/$_2$ cups crushed graham crackers

^{1}/$_2$ cup butter

1 14 oz can Eagle Brand sweetened condensed milk

2 cups (12 oz) semi-sweet chocolate chips

1^1/$_3$ cups flaked coconut

1 cup chopped pecan or walnuts

1. Preheat oven to 350 degrees.
2. In a small bowl combine graham cracker crumbs and butter; mix well and press crumb mixture firmly on bottom of the 13 x 9 Baking dish.
3. Pour sweetened condensed milk evenly over crumbs.
4. Layer evenly with remaining ingredients: Chocolate chips (or butterscotch or peanut butter chips-they are all delicious), nuts and coconut flakes.
5. Press down firmly with a fork.
6. In a 350 degree oven, bake magic bars for 25 minutes or until lightly browned. Cool. Cut into squares or bars.

Serve.

Every May we have strawberries. There is nothing like a fresh from the garden strawberry. The Cabbage Patch is the name of the local farm that grows and harvests strawberries. Those berries are delicious and we buy many flats of them for strawberry shortcake and to freeze for winter's oatmeal. But mostly we like strawberries for the Strawberry Pie.

Strawberry Pie

1 9-inch pie shell

4 cups fresh strawberries, cleaned, sliced and divided

1 cup sugar

1 cup water

3 tablespoon cornstarch

$\frac{1}{2}$ teaspoon salt

1 teaspoon butter

1 cup whipped cream

1. In a small saucepan mix 2 cups of strawberries, sugar, water, cornstarch and salt. Cook until thick.
2. Remove from heat, add butter and stir well. Cool.
3. Put the 2 remaining cups of strawberries in the baked pie shell. Pour glaze over berries. Refrigerate until serving time.
4. Cut into slices and add whipped cream.

Serve.

Southern Pecan Pie

1 prepared deep-dish pie shell

3 eggs, slightly beaten

1 cup sugar

1 cup Karo Syrup—Dark or Light (this recipe is from the
     bottle of Karo Syrup)

2 tablespoons butter, melted

1 teaspoon vanilla

1¼ cup chopped pecans

1. Preheat the oven to 350 degrees.
2. Mix the eggs, sugar, syrup, butter and vanilla.
3. Add the pecans and mix.
4. Pour mixture into pie shell and cook at 350 degrees for 50
   minutes or until an inserted toothpick comes out clean.
5. When you take it out of the oven let it cool for 30 to 40
   minutes.

Serve.

My Grandmother, Maude Martin was a great cook. She made Parker House Rolls that were beyond delicious. When they were served at her dining room table, place settings for sixteen and each person took one roll, the table was silent because they were warm, soft, melty, full of flavor and awesomely delicious. They were eaten with great appreciation.

Grandmother took great pride in her cooking and she taught my Mom how to cook after Mom married her oldest son, my Dad. Mom tells the story about right after they first married and had moved into a tiny apartment in DeWitt, Virginia how every morning she'd measure exactly two cups of water and put it on to boil to make their instant coffee. She could never figure out why she didn't have enough water for two cups when she poured it. Mom had never cooked.

On my daughter Lisa's third birthday I made her a cake that my Grandmother had made for special occasions ever since I could remember. She gave me the recipe and I titled it: Grandmother Maude's Orange Chiffon Cake. Lisa loved it so much that for every birthday thereafter I made Grandmother's Orange Chiffon Cake.

Grandmother Maude's Orange Chiffon Cake

You'll need two ungreased 9-inch cake pans

2¼ cups all-purpose flour

1½ cups sugar

3 teaspoons baking powder

1 teaspoon salt

½ cup vegetable oil

8 egg yolks

8 egg whites

½ teaspoon cream of tartar

¾ cups fresh squeezed orange juice

3 tablespoons grated orange rind

1. Preheat the oven to 325 degrees.
2. Sift together the flour, sugar, baking powder and salt. Make a well in the center of the bowl and add the oil. Mix thoroughly.
3. Separate the eggs. Whisk the yolks together.
4. Add the egg whites to a large bowl, add the cream of tartar, and whip until stiff peaks form.
5. Pour the egg yolks over the egg whites and gently fold the two ingredients together until completely mixed.
6. Add the dry ingredients to the eggs in batches, mixing thoroughly between each addition.
7. Add the juice and zest and mix in gently. Divide the batter equally among the pans.
8. Bake in two ungreased pans at 325 degrees for 65 minutes.
9. Cool and frost.

Frosting:

Juice of one orange

$\frac{1}{2}$ stick butter

$1\frac{1}{2}$ cups sugar

1. Put all the ingredients in a small saucepan and bring to a boil. Boil just enough to form soft ball in water. (In a mug of room temperature water, drop a spoonful of the cooking frosting. When you can roll it into a soft ball in the water, it's ready to cool for your cake.)
2. Let it cool a bit then spread over cake.

Serve.

A Lot of Learning Going On

I've been on a spiritual quest for a long time. Really, ever since I can remember, I had questions about why we're here and the meaning of life. I questioned the Bible. I wanted to know who really wrote it and, when they were copying it from language to language, did they always copy exactly. I asked this of a Primitive Baptist preacher when I was around 10 or 11 and he listened intently, then he looked at Mom and asked if she'd take me out of the room and she did. That was a lesson which I took to heart. Don't question authority.

As a young woman living in Richmond, I visited all types of churches and was prayed over, spoke in tongues, went to Quaker meetings where I didn't say a word, attended a Jewish Synagogue and had gefilte fish stuffed in my mouth (never went back to that one) and to a Presbyterian Church where I met a group of ladies who studied the Bible. Seriously studied it. They came to the Friday morning meetings prepared. They always had their faithful tattered Bibles, but also history books, scholarly texts and minister's sermons. They wore gloves and hats—sweet proper Virginia ladies. Thank God they also had their own strong opinions and didn't mind sharing them. After our morning class on Fridays, we adjourned to the Tearoom at Miller and Rhodes Department Store for the fashion show and chicken salad plate. It was a very civilized way of life.

It was through these ladies I met Dr. George Ritchie, the person who truly changed my life. Dr. Ritchie was tall, with coal black hair and dark eyes. He emanated a powerful persona.

From George Ritchie I learned that there is no death; that we can easily do what Jesus did (easy for George to say after raising a man from the dead). George was a physician but realized that patients in the 60s were coming to him, not with physical pains, but with emotional and spiritual pains. He returned to the University of Virginia and studied psychiatry. I went to see him as a patient and had huge realizations; I finally understood many of the decisions I'd made and why I'd made them. I learned that it is okay to start over and that just because I formed an opinion did not mean I couldn't change my mind (that was especially hard). Or that just because I'd "made my bed hard, I did not have to lie in it." Most of all, I realized that I was then and now surrounded with extraordinary people and that I could trust them.

George said, when you realize you've made a mistake, you're a fool if you keep on with it. Acknowledge it, work on it, pray on it, then deal with it, forgive and move on. For God's sake, he'd say, don't keep on with the mistake. All you're doing, when you live with a mistake, is making more karma, going deeper and deeper in the psyche.

A.R.E. in Virginia Beach was a hotbed of discussion about our ancient and true origins, how our beliefs shape who we are, and our understanding of why we're here. Edgar Cayce's readings rang true to me from the first book I read. He'd died in 1945 but in the late 1960s, Jess Stearn had written a book, *The Sleeping Prophet* and it'd become a bestseller.

Everyone who was anyone in the New Age field spoke at A.R.E. One of the best speakers at that time, the 80's, was Richard Bach. He'd written: *Jonathan Livingston Seagull*. He shared his understanding of consciousness based on that most famous book. He was so surprised that so many people came to hear him that he said he'd stay as long as we wanted to hear him speak. He started at 8 PM and he spoke until 4 AM.

I listened to knowledgeable speakers on Edgar Cayce's 14,000 readings: Shirley Winston "toned" and sang to us about music and altered states; Edgar Evans Cayce talked about his "home town" of Atlantis; Mark Thurston presented Cayce's information on the soul's journey; Henry Reed led us in dream workshops; Everett Irion seriously researched The Book of Revelation; Herb Puryear preached on Spirituality; Hugh Lynn Cayce with his twinkling blue eyes told stories about his Dad; and Nell Clairemont taught us meditation; Elsie Sechrist spoke and wrote a book on dreams and on and on. Most people won't know any of these authors but the ones who do will remember them with love and a grateful heart.

During the decades from the late 60s, through the 70s and 80s, I absorbed every morsel of knowledge I could take in from A.R.E. speakers. They had generous spirits and their talks were always lovingly presented. I couldn't get enough.

After speakers expanded my horizons, I'd sit for hours with friends and often with the speakers going over details of the talk, often with rousing discussions. First, we sat in rocking chairs on the front porch of the original A.R.E. hospital building, then across the street at the cafeteria of the oceanfront Marshall's Hotel and later we'd sit at The Jewish Mother, a restaurant down on Pacific Avenue a couple of miles from A.R.E.

It was mentally invigorating and spiritually inspiring, stretching the borders of what I knew or thought I knew and confirming so many concepts and ideas that I'd puzzled over. Every piece of information seemed to be to be something that I already somehow knew. I finally realized that my reaction was a re-hearing, a reminder of ancient wisdom wrapped in new clothes.

I was like an intellectual and spiritual sponge. I wanted to know everything.

When I first moved to New York City, I had extensive and deep discussions with people like Michael Grosso, who'd written *The Final Choice: Playing the Survival Game*. Michael was a philosophy professor, deep thinker and an excellent writer. In my copy of his book, almost every sentence of *Final Choice* is underlined. His writing was so empowering and spoke to me so strongly that I called him and said I wanted to meet him. This was during the time I was driving from Virginia Beach to Manhattan and staying here and there. That time I was down near the Bowery and Michael lived in Riverdale, a little north of Manhattan. He took many subways and an hour to get all the way to this little diner where we talked for many hours. I was in heaven.

Michael's newest book is *The Man Who Could Fly: St. Joseph of Copertino and the Mystery of Levitation*. An excellent book.

What have I learned? That life as we know it is an illusion. That our experiences are meant to correct old patterns, start new ones and mend ways with loved and hated companions. We have choices. What we decide every minute creates our future, moment by moment. We come in with a "plan" but sometimes we pay no attention to it; sometimes our childhood circumstances make it impossible to follow the plan, and other times we follow it to the letter. Dreams are a window into the past and the future if you are open to them. I have met and know people who are living in multiple dimensions simultaneously. The physical body is merely a cup-holder for the spirit. Our souls, our spirits are more powerful and magnificent than we can even imagine. There is no death.

Most importantly: the only real thing, the most important thing is love; loving one another without judgment.

After being a New Yorker, I'd wanted to move back to Virginia Beach where I knew lots of like-minded thinkers in my genre. I applied for a job at A.R.E, but they didn't hire me so I ended up living full time in Bracey, for real, for good.

Being here with my good friends, my beautiful garden, and even with all my ups and downs, has enabled me to write this "delicious" book and share a few stories from my life.

This is only a tiny sampling, but I am grateful to have the opportunity to sit and talk with you.

Acknowledgments

I have admired writers since I learned to read. As a little girl growing up on a farm, books were the gift that sent my mind soaring. What it takes to write a well thought out, carefully written manuscript is never fully appreciated until you've done it yourself. Now I understand. Barbara Lagowski and Beth Wareham have my thanks for their editorial and creative suggestions and for Laura Smyth's design of the book.

I am grateful that Lisa Hagan's idea for me to write a cookbook actually materialized. Thank you Lisa for the loving and gracious way you guided me though this process.

Sandra Martin

Sandra Martin's career as a literary agent and executive producer for television has been devoted to bringing inspiring, boundary breaking books and television documentaries in the fields of spirituality, self-help and consciousness to the mainstream public.

In 1986 Ms. Martin created Paraview, Inc. Paraview holds a unique position in the media industry for being among the first to successfully develop literary properties for the worldwide audience of "Cultural Creatives"—a 50 million+ audience interested in consciousness, deep spirituality, healing and the paranormal.

As a literary agent Ms. Martin had many books on the *New York Times* bestsellers list. During the 90s she was one of the first agents to develop and launch her own imprint, Paraview Books. In 2000 she negotiated a deal with Simon and Schuster to create a new imprint, Paraview Pocket Books, a division of Simon and Schuster Publishing.

Ms. Martin also created and executive produced a three hour documentary series for the Discovery Channel titled *The Power of Dreams*, and for PBS a three hour documentary series, *Intuition* for the PBS Pledge Fund Drive. As executive producer for *Is it really me?* she was awarded a CINE Golden Eagle Award.

In 2002, she accepted the position of Senior Vice President of Content for Wisdom Television. At Wisdom she was responsible for developing and producing programming for the new linear cable channel. Programming at Wisdom included; *Wisdom at Work, A Wisdom Holiday: The Gift of Song, Is It Really Me? Loretta La Roche—Life is Not a Stress Rehearsal*. At Sirius Radio in New York City, a critical and profound discussion on the spiritual aspects of life after the World Trade Center attack was filmed. It was titled, *9.11.02: From the Ground Up*, Hosted by Caroline Myss and Jim Garrison.

Ms. Martin has served on the boards of Friends for the Institute of Noetic Sciences in New York City, The Rhine Research Center and the International Association for Near Death Studies in Durham, North Carolina, Harvard University's Center for Psychology and Social Change and NurturArt of New York City.

As a consultant, Ms. Martin worked with Time Life Books on their best selling series, *Mysteries of the Unknown*; Berkley Bedell's National Foundation for Alternative Medicine, now called Foundation for Alternative and Integrative Medicine and The Mountain Institute.

Made in the USA
Columbia, SC
20 January 2020